Praise for *It's Only A Candy Bar*

"For years I have told anyone that would listen that as Christians we can see the true fruit of our labor when someone we have had the privilege of bringing to Christ goes out and brings Christ to others. So often we pat ourselves on the back and yet we are only effective when our fruit reproduces itself. At the heart of this story is the investment it takes to disciple others and how our greatest joy in serving Christ comes not from what we do but from what those we invest in do.

"Evan Gratz has shown us how ministry can be difficult and challenging. Through his relationship with Tyler we also see the reward of ministry when someone Evan has invested in has gone on 'to do even greater things than I have done' (John 14:12). A high school student finds his faith and a youth minister is reminded that God gets the credit for the growth."

> **Gayla Cooper Congdon**
> **Founder/Chief Spiritual Officer**
> **Amor Ministries**

"Evan is deeply passionate about teenagers and that is evident in every word of this book. Youth workers are convinced that the world can be changed for good by young people who grab on to God's word and live that out. This is true for Evan and his story about the journey of a youth pastor and student is a display of this exciting reality."

> **Angie Horn-Andreu**
> **Sr. Director of Guest Experience**
> **Forest Home Mill Creek Canyon**

"It's truly more than a Candy Bar! It is a gift every youth pastor, youth leader, and pastor should read! It is a sweet reminder how precious students are to the Lord and how important adults are in their lives."

> **Gordon Gathright**
> **Lifelong Youth Ministry Vet**

"One of the most challenging questions for Christian leaders in today's society has to be: How can we reach the next generation for Christ? Youth ministry plays a vital role in presenting the gospel in such a way that it will penetrate through the calloused hearts of today's young adults. Evan Gratz gives us an emotional glimpse into what building relationships with youth can require. In the story, *It's Only A Candy Bar*, Evan's vulnerability takes you on an emotional rollercoaster between a minister and young adult. Evan's words will carry you on a journey through the fruits of the Spirit, through love and marriage, pain and tragedy, and boldly through the redemption and salvation of Christ. This is a special story that I hope many will experience. That you too will be inspired to reach this generation for Christ."

> **Ben Utecht**
> **Super Bowl XLI Champion Tight End for the**
> **Indianapolis Colts and**
> **Christian Recording Artist**

"For many years, Evan Gratz has been building relationships with young people, leading them to Christ and guiding them into a deeper relationship with their faith walk. Using a novel format in *It's Only A Candy Bar*, he engages the reader from the opening page and the reader sees the struggles and joys of working with teens. This story is filled with twists and unexpected turns yet based on the author's real life experiences. More than a novel, this book includes a series of pointed questions for an individual or a small group to use the book as a discussion starter.

"Every youth worker will be able to see glimpses of their own work and gain insight into their own work through reading this book. Teenage readers will also benefit from this book because they will see that life is filled with unexpected twists and challenges with only One relationship which is key and lasting: Jesus. The perfect book for any Christian who works with teens. Recommended."

> **Terry Whalin**
> **Publisher and Author of over 60 books**

It's Only A Candy Bar

*A high school student finds faith
and a youth pastor renews his own*

By
Evan Gratz

Intermedia Publishing Group

It's Only A Candy Bar

Published by:
Intermedia Publishing Group, Inc.
P.O. Box 2825
Peoria, Arizona 85380
www.intermediapub.com

ISBN 978-1-935906-03-2

Edited by JoHanna Gratz.

Dedication

**For my wife, JoHanna,
and Mom and Dad**

**In memory of Grandma and Grandpa Gratz,
and Grandma Nielsen**

In honor of Grandpa Nielsen

Table of Contents

Acknowledgements

God—For your grace and guidance of my life.

JoHanna—For your faith, love and patience in joining me in this adventure! You are loved and adored so deeply.

Mom and Dad—For your continuous love and support throughout far too many choices, dreams and ideas I've had.

My family—For helping to build me up and shaping me into the person that I am.

All of my friends who mean everything to me. Thanks for all of the love, realness and conversations. You are all the best! You know who you are…

Gordon Gathright—For being such an inspiring example of the kingdom and how to love teenagers and people. You are one of the "Fathers" of youth ministry and are a huge reason I have felt called to do what I do.

All of the mentors who I have had over the years for your teaching, guidance and love. I hope you know how much it's meant.

To coffee shops and fast food restaurants everywhere for providing such great opportunities to minister to students!

To "In N Out" for being incredible.

To all of you who I've had the privilege and honor of partnering with in the trenches of youth ministry! What a crazy ride! **Volunteers, leaders and staff.**

The memory of Greg Lips. One of my closest friends who helped shape my faith during very pivotal years in my life. "E and G up on Kenwood."

Heart Behind The Book

God doesn't need us, he *wants* us. This can sometimes be a crazy thought, but one that can offer direction and a purpose in our lives. I grew up learning a lot about the church and who Jesus was, but it took me awhile to really understand and get who Jesus IS. Once I figured that out, things started to change in my life. And I knew that it didn't have as much to do with the knowledge I was gaining through learning, but the learning I was gaining through other people investing in me. Through the relationships in my personal life, I came to really know Jesus and how to relate to Him. It's not much different than with the people I have had around me throughout my life.

I guess that's why it's been easier for me to make that connection to students and others, because it makes sense to me. By building relationships we grow in knowledge but also in character. I struggled for a lot of years trying to figure out what I wanted to be when I grew up. I'm still kind of there, but I at least know that I want to invest the rest of my life into the lives of high school students in whatever capacity God calls.

God doesn't need us to do His will on earth, but he wants us, and for some reason He uses our lives to connect Himself with others. I don't think there's a more rewarding feeling than investing your life in something that God has deemed good and worthy. For me, that's been the lives of teenagers.

I wanted to be a professional athlete growing up, and have had dreams of being an actor and even a phase of wanting to be in a boy band. (I'm still hopeful for a shot at that one someday.) I have always wanted to be a teacher as well, but it seemed that no matter what I felt I wanted to do, God was shaping all of those elements into something different: A career in youth ministry.

Youth ministry is a funny thing. I've been doing it full-time or as a volunteer within the church and through Young Life for over ten years. And every day I straddle the line between turning away from it all or whole-heartedly following it for the rest of my life! What a RUSH! I feel that's how life needs to be lived. It's a wild ride! It's as Mike Yaconelli says, a "Wild Abandon." And at the end of it all, I know all I want to say is that I've been faithful and lived my life the way it was intended to be lived. Youth ministry is so much more than eating pizza, reading the Bible and singing "Kumbaya."

I'm not a writer. But I have always wanted to write and act in my own movie, so I guess that's what this book is. I woke up one night with a vision. I had a movie script play through my mind and I spent an hour in the middle of the night telling my wife what I had visioned. So, the next week I just started writing. I had a story and I wanted to tell it. I have heard that you write about what you know and you write how you speak, that's what I've done with *It's Only A Candy Bar*. It became an outlet and journal for me to write about the frustrations and passions I've dealt with in my years of youth ministry. There was a distinct sense of release as I wrote this book, as if I could start breathing slowly again.

My prayer for this book is that this story will inspire and convict you by giving you a chance to evaluate your own life and purpose. I'm not content to live a life of boredom and I don't want to just live, get fat, die and rot. We're created for far more importance than that! There's a God who holds this all together, and no matter how we're feeling at any given moment, God is constantly calling us to a life of purpose and meaning. I pray you find that or are renewed in your own.

Everyone's life tells a story… What's yours?

Evan
www.evangratz.com
Follow Evan on twitter @evangratz

1

Starting Fresh Out West

"Faith is taking the first step even when you can't
see the whole staircase."
– Martin Luther King Jr.

"Dude, I gotta go."

"What? We were just heading over to Pete's house," Luke said with the anticipation felt only by a seventeen-year-old senior.

"Where are you going?" he continued as they stood against the wall outside of a Taco Bell.

"Just this family thing my parents want me at," Tyler responded with a tone that was obviously lying and hiding something. He felt the questioning look from Luke, as he said,

"Right, that's bull, what are you really doing?" The death look almost turned into satisfaction as if he'd pushed his buddy up against the wall and knew the answer would give him some leverage because of the humiliation Tyler felt. With high schoolers it's always a competition, especially between friends. You could almost sense the ridicule going through Luke's mind before Tyler even spoke again.

Tyler lifted his head up, making sure to avoid eye contact, and said, "Just this thing at my church my parents are making me go to; some new youth guy is coming or something, but it'll be lame and I'm just doing it so I can go out this weekend," he said, speeding up his words with the last phrase there, I'm sure to justify the embarrassment. Luke looked blankly back at Tyler, almost confused and said, "Dude, what? You go to church?"

Tyler flicked the rest of his cigarette at Luke's face, punched him on the arm and said, "Your mom goes to church..." then walked away.

This is one of those conversations that I would have loved to been a fly on the wall for. Especially knowing Tyler as he is today. It almost makes me laugh at the insecurity and uncertainty which I'd bet was radiating from him. I'm sure he'd tell you the same.

I remember that first meeting well; having moved all the way from Minnesota, dragging my wife, JoHanna, across the

country in two vehicles, a moving truck and filling the second bedroom of our new/old, small apartment only the night before with all of our belongings. Apparently California didn't believe in garages, or basements for that matter. We had a chance to meet the congregation, shake hands and kiss the babies etc. that morning at the church services. Now was the night to meet the students, their parents, and hopefully get a better glimpse of why we felt God was "calling" me to a position in Southern California.

I remember sitting in a cramped and stuffy room feeling exhausted, missing my friends and family, and looking at JoHanna as she tried as usual to put on a smile and happy face. Even though I was certain she was feeling a lot of the same things I was. Was this really happening? Out of all of the options, opportunities and possibilities, here we were; this was our decision.

The meeting went all right. It started off with an opening prayer, that let's be honest, sometimes feels much more forced than an actual conversation with God. But it moved on into my introduction which actually made me sound pretty sweet. The head of the youth search team spoke and introduced me as "Evan, our answer to a year-long extensive search." He shared about all of the volunteer work I'd done, mission trips I'd led, schooling, skills and experience I had. It made me sound like Father Teresa. Part of me was feeling uncomfortable, but there was another part of me that was curious if they were going to start talking about all of the orphanages and schools I'd built in Africa, and how I'd saved a remote colony of starving children and their families and put them through school. In my head no matter what was being said was leading to a million expectations.

I was quickly learning throughout that meeting, that I was possibly getting in over my head. Here I was staring at a room full of parents and students, who were telling me all about their lives, histories, expectations and stories, and how I was this answer to prayer. Yet in reality, all my gut kept telling me was that I didn't care about their stories and I didn't think I wanted to be in ministry at all anymore!

After the meeting was over, I met some more of the students. Funny how I hadn't seen any of them at even one of the three services that morning. But they were your typical kids: flirting awkwardly, jockeying for social status position, (especially within their own youth group) and throwing elbows at each other for an opportunity to tell me all about themselves. Each one had their own unique way of communicating. Some were mature, some were quiet and some were insensitive, like when they tried to make my wife and I say the words "boat" and "bagel" over and over, just to hear our Minnesota accents.

But they were kids. They were the reason I moved across the country, they were the reason I had this passion for teaching. There had always been something so fragile, innocent and real about where high school students are at in life. It's almost like they hadn't experienced routine and disappointment yet and still felt that anything was possible and there was no challenge too big. That's the kind of energy I found myself drawn to. I found myself conflicted between getting inspired, through inspiring students to change the world for the kingdom of God, and just letting it all go and crawling into a cave; or in this case a small apartment, and never stepping foot into a church again.

Before I left that meeting, I saw a couple of parents talking. I noticed that behind them was a kid wearing a hoodie and skinny jeans, listening to his ipod and texting on his iphone. He was sitting on a brick wall outside the church doors. He had longer brown hair that covered most of his eyes and was about five foot ten, the same size as me, except for being about twenty-five pounds lighter. And of course, he happened to be in my exact line of traffic heading toward our car. I smiled at the parents who seemed to be in a great "parking lot" conversation, probably gossiping about one of the other parents or discussing how one of the youth group kids is ruining things for everyone else; those types of discussions. But as I got closer to this kid, something happened. Nothing. Yeah, instead of the eager affection I'd been receiving as the center of attention, there was no acknowledgement what-so-ever.

So I leaned down and put my fist in front of him for a fist pound. He obliged by lightly and very briefly pounding my hand as his head turned up toward me, only for a split second. I don't even know if that would count as eye contact, but regardless, there was a reaction. I uttered something like "Keep it real, bro," as I started walking away, knowing full well that he didn't hear me, considering I could hear every word, or scream rather, to the song blaring through the personal ear buds on his ipod.

That was the first time I met Tyler. I figured it would maybe be my last, for a variety of reasons, but there was something God was doing in the both of us that I wouldn't see or recognize until later.

JoHanna and I got into our car and drove the twenty minutes home to our apartment that night. There are those pivotal moments in our lives, when we have "ah-hah" moments; we seem to *get it* and our path is clear and it all makes sense! This was not one of those times. This was the opposite. This was an "oh crap, what did we do?" time.

It was silent for about five minutes. There wasn't tension between us, but there was this sort of silent, internal moment of debriefing, where we knew we were thinking the same thing. I finally turned my head very slightly to catch her out of the corner of my eye and she had a single tear rolling down her face. She was sitting in silence, her usual beautiful smile gone, her brown hair and bangs pushed to the side of her face as her petite, energetic body and livelihood gave way to her true feelings in that moment. My heart sank into my stomach, liver, appendix and every other organ in my body as I felt lost. The road could've been water and the car a sailboat drifting without a direction for as little control as I had on my own life that night. But being human, I was overwhelmed by the responsibility I had to control it all. I looked forward in a stare and said in a quiet and questioning voice, "What are we doing here? If this is all part of God's plan, why are we feeling like this?"

That night I couldn't sleep. My mind was going crazy with everything that was going on. I had baggage and hurt from the past, I had drama, and I had a wife who I was trying to take care of and nurture, and now I had just begun a job where the primary role is to build relationships and listen to all of those same things in others. How could I get myself to a point where I cared enough to try?

And then, the image of Tyler popped into my head. I think that bothered me more than anything that night. It was subtle, but after coming off a high of everyone praising me and giving me attention, it felt like he didn't care at all. And by not affirming me or showing me worth, it drove me and my "people pleasing" nature crazy. I said a prayer that night and told God that if He wanted me to reach out to this kid, to give me the strength and also the opportunity; like it or not, we were in California and we were staying for a while.

2

The School Lunch Experiment

"It's good to do uncomfortable things.
It's weight training for life."
– Anne Lamott, *Plan B: Further Thoughts on Faith*

The next day, which was my first full day in the office, I noticed a lot of things. Gone were the comforts and privacy I had at my last position in Minnesota. I was in a cubicle with a computer that was formerly and presently used by volunteers and I was also surrounded by a few other staff people in the room. I missed my Mac and I wanted to check Facebook. There wasn't a whole lot there to work with, but I found a shelf full of books all about youth ministry that were probably published twenty years ago before I was even in high school. I got a good laugh from looking through a few of them, as I rocked and swirled in the squeaky black office chair. It was a great reminder about how far youth ministry has come, but also comforting to know a lot of things never change. However, something that *had* changed was the culture and clothing worn in some of those pictures. Really? Faded, white-washed jeans, Zubaz, mullets galore and everyone's teeth were the natural off-white color. What's that about?

It was like using those textbooks in high school where the pictures are so outdated and the books are torn, chipped and ripped up, yet the teacher still makes you use a book cover. For me I would always be the last to do it, and eventually have my mom use a grocery bag from Cub Foods to complete the deed.

The reality was that I was in shock. I knew what I was doing overall; I had a lot of experience and training as far as working with students, but this new job would need some adjusting. I had a brief panic attack then did what every youth pastor in my situation would have done that day; I bailed and went to Starbucks about mid-morning. I love the idea and ambience of coffee shops, but I am kind of a poser when it comes to drinking it. I really don't like it. I'm the guy that'll buy the most non-coffee drink there, like a frappuccino, take a few sips then throw the rest away.

While I was sitting there in the empty Starbucks, a lot was going through my head. I was a bit more optimistic and less emotional than I was the previous night, and I knew JoHanna was too. I had settled down some in that way, but I knew something was going to have to happen in order for me to feel as though this situation was justified. While I struggled with trying to plan the next few months of activities for students I barely knew, I couldn't get the thought of Tyler and his burn of me out of my mind.

So impulsively I grabbed my keys and headed to the local high school. It was the end of summer/beginning of fall, so school had just started about two weeks prior. You could see and feel that it was a new school year. The guys' Axe deodorant was nauseating already, twenty feet before entering the campus, signs were plastered all over school with ads for the new clubs, pep rally stuff for sports teams and voting for the upcoming homecoming royalty; all that fun high school stuff.

After signing in at the office, I started walking toward the lunch area where the next wave of students would be coming in any minute. Now, this wasn't anything new to me, I'd been on high school campuses a lot before with coaching and hanging out with students in general, but this was different. In California, lunch is more of a zone than it is a confined indoor cell as I remember growing up. Little pockets and groups of students covered a pretty large outdoor radius and there weren't coaches and teachers barricading the exits. This intimidated me a little, however, because I couldn't find the right spot to hang out at and pray a student would come up to me and say hello. I only wanted to be a presence, not necessarily go as far as having a full-on conversation with anyone.

I lingered for a bit and finally got some courage; I went up to a table of a few students and asked, "Hey, when is lunch over?" I'm sure that seemed creepy to them that a twenty-nine-year-old random stranger with a visitor's pass, short messy blonde hair, a perpetual 5 o'clock shadow, who'd been sulking by himself for ten minutes, would just come up to them. I felt like I was in eighth grade all over again at a dance, nervously waiting for a response as if I'd just asked the girl of my dreams to dance with me in front of all my friends and peers. The response wasn't flattering. It was simple and concise. One of the kids who must have been their leader looked at me with a sharp tone and two lip rings and said "F--- You, man," which he gracefully unedited for my ears.

It wasn't sincere, it was instinct. It came from a different place and I'd been around students enough to know that it wasn't about me at all. I quickly shrugged it off and said, "Great way to talk man," then walked away shaking my head and left the lunch area. In a moment like that, there wasn't a right thing to say. Anything out of my mouth would've been mocked. It took a lot of maturity on my part not to tell him what I really thought, or react how I would've back when I was in high school if he'd said that to me. But either way, I left.

I started wondering why I was there, what I was doing, and why I was putting myself through those kinds of experiences willingly. But before I could wallow in self-pity much longer, I noticed a few guys chillin' by my ride, or for the culturally inept; "standing near my car." They weren't there intentionally, trust me. It had to have been an accident, coincidence, or fate. *Now,* the last thing I wanted was to be noticed. It made it worse that I was totally dressed like a high school kid with plaid shorts, a Volcom shirt and flip flops. One girl that day actually asked what grade I was in, but then another asked me if I had a child in high school, so I guess they canceled each other out.

What was cool though, was that in this group of four or five guys, I saw Tyler. He was laughing, swearing and smoking with his buddies. He had more of an athletic build and confidence that I hadn't noticed the first time, and I thought to myself, "Awesome. Here's my shot." So I casually strolled up to their crew; because let's face it, I had nothing left to lose, and said, "Tyler, what's going on today, brother?" I can only imagine what was going through his head at that moment; embarrassment, shock and many other emotions I am sure. I'm also sure he knew if he was nice to me, he'd get a lot of crap from his friends, but if he wasn't, his parents would hear about it. What a dilemma for an insecure high school student! I loved it since I'm a guy that strives in uncomfortable situations anyway.

His response was simply, "Hey." A little more chipper than the night before, but the conversation and laughter between the guys went completely dull.

I tried to make small talk for a minute, asking questions about classes, sports, movies and whatever came to mind. The answers I got back were very short, one-word answers. As the bell rang, they all said in unison "We gotta head…" I could see it was a huge relief and out for them. I've always been of the respectful mindset not to put a kid down or embarrass them unless you know for a fact they can take it in a joking manner and dish it out too, so that's why this next part was a guess.

As they walked away, everything in me said, shut up, don't say it, but I did, pretty dang loudly too, "Hey Tyler, hope to see you at church this week! Oh and bring your buddies!" I heard some snickering as I turned to head to my car, knowing I'd gotten some sort of mini-redemption from him snubbing me the night before.

Needless to say, I didn't see Tyler or his friends at church that week, or any of the following weeks, but I set that aside for a while because I needed to focus on getting settled in to my new life.

Over the next couple of weeks I found myself really starting to embrace California in the way I originally hoped I would. JoHanna and I would go for walks, take trips to the beach, find little Farmers' Markets, all of those nice little romantic things. I even bought a pair of Rainbow sandals which I was told made me a real native. More often than not we were acting like tourists, taking pictures of everything. I mean it was after all, the Golden State, where dreams came true. Our lives were starting to adjust to our new environment, and it didn't take much of a struggle to adapt to the climate. Actually, after the first month of being in California, I forgot what rain and clouds looked like. There was much more optimism in our voices and conversations, but still an over-arching theme of, "What's next?"

We had both had great experiences and opportunities in life, but they seemed brief, especially on the job front. I'm not sure if it's because we got bored easily, or just always felt that we *could* be doing something different, therefore we needed to. We have always had a consistent feeling of being unsettled, yet ironically desired to settle down more than anything. We always thought things would be better somewhere else, the "grass is always greener" philosophy. Yet deep down, now, I was running in fear that my life wouldn't ever settle and that I wouldn't do anything of significance because I was such a rolling stone. And it didn't help that JoHanna felt the same way, so we were both constantly trying to take flight while hoping the other would keep us grounded.

One of the things in my personal life that I was learning, was how to down-size my social network. Part of my gift mix is that I am a very relational person. I really love people and strive in social environments. I have always been the proverbial LOP (Life of the Party), it has been a trait since I was young. In high school I played sports, was in band, student council, sang in the choir and did pretty much anything else that would keep me and my ADHD occupied. Through those activities I made a lot of friends. Then, because of my rolling stone mindset, I transferred colleges twice, while each time bringing and expanding a social network like I was the Verizon Wireless guy. Many of the people I knew were acquaintances, but there were also many that I had invested significantly in.

Since I was such a people pleaser I had this mind frame that wouldn't allow me to let a lot of those friendships drift away. I felt compelled to spend time keeping contact and trying to stay close with everyone, when all that ended up happening was I got to a place where I wasn't very close to a few, but I was moderately close with a lot. A bunch of lukewarm friendships that weren't all that fulfilling. So what I had been doing was dwindling down my relationships to the couple handfuls of people that I chose to invest in long-term. Man, Jesus had it right with His crew of twelve disciples!

Much of this seemed timely considering we were in an entirely new place and had to start campaigning for friends and building new relationships. Sure there was texting, cell phones, Skype and e-mail to keep contact with family and friends far away, but we needed some instant gratification. And for anyone who's late twenties and older and has ever moved far away from their home base could tell you that it's tough to meet friends at that stage in life. We realized that our three hot spots for friends were going to be Church, Work and Community Activities. However, that formula didn't suit us very well. I *worked* AT a *church*, so those canceled each other out, and because of the nature of building relationships in my job, it was hard to do much else after getting home. Almost like having to see one more cup of coffee at home when you leave your long work day at the coffee shop. It became more of a chore than anything and that was how our life in California started off in the beginning—it was a chore.

Back to the job situation; JoHanna didn't have one. We joked that her full-time job was finding a job, except it wasn't a very funny joke considering the stress involved in looking and the fact that we were living off the ever prestigious and fat youth pastor's salary I was receiving. There aren't too many people that enter ministry for the money, which I guess is a good thing.

My job, however, really started out as more of an actual job. Like I said before, I was put into a cubical with five other people in a room that was the size of my bedroom growing up, which wasn't big. I was a hard worker, but being confined in such a small space brought back harsh reminders of when I worked in the corporate world for all of six months after college. After those six months I vowed to never do it again. But the silver lining with that job was I'd learned how to pass the time, look busy and do just enough work so no one would bother me. Church work was different though, it was something I understood and was good and passionate about. I knew how to manage my time and didn't need someone looking over my shoulder or micro-managing. Slowly I started to branch out and spend more and more time at the coffee shop or in the youth room. I spent my first couple of weeks putting together a calendar of events and planning some cool trips and retreats as we started youth group off that fall with a bang. Literally.

3

The Broken Breakdown

"All the emotion I'd felt over the past month,
the excitement, sorrow, questioning, everything
came to a head and I realized that this entire move,
my entire life had nothing to do with me."
– Evan Gratz

I'm not sure what age we stop being cool, but I definitely think it's a certain number, not just a mindset. I'm actually looking forward to getting there, so I don't have to try so hard. As for now I hope I'm still caught on the good side of being cool around teenagers.

My first official youth group night that fall went pretty well. I had moved out all of the pews in the traditional looking sanctuary and blasted music over the speakers. I had put together a playlist with some old classic dance songs like "Thriller," "YMCA," and "Down Under" by Men at Work. I also slyly mixed in a few worship songs. A little after 7 p.m. the kids started showing up, all thirteen of them that night which was pretty good since it was a school night and none of them knew me yet. I counted that as a win.

I started out with a game called "Animal" where we'd go around in a circle and each person was to be a different animal and could only speak by doing their animal sound and action. Similar to an old Young Life game I knew called "Big Booty." It got weird, which I guess was the point. Then, that game turned into a few more games I had put together which were reminiscent of *American Gladiators*. It was complete with an obstacle course, and a few others, but we ended with a game of war. I had put out about 100 balls from a ball crawl you'd see at Chuck E. Cheese's and we split the sanctuary into two sides. The object was to throw as many balls to the opponent's side within two minutes. The side with the least balls on their side at the end would win. It got chaotic, but was okay since the balls were very light and harmless. However, we had been using tennis balls for the previous game, and since kids don't always listen, before I knew it, there were a few kids chucking tennis balls at each other across the room.

Did I mention that the walls on both sides were made up entirely of glass?

Well, as you can imagine, there was a window that got completely shattered, on my first youth group night. I thought it was kind of funny, but was freaking out when I had to call the pastor to take care of it.

After we ended, there were a few kids lingering outside waiting for a ride. They were high on energy and I felt good about the night. I started to think it was going to be all right. Then it hit me. And by "it," I mean this kid, Landon. He was tall, had a constant smile and a big, curly blonde fro. He came up to me and said with an endearing, yet serious tone, "Hey man, tonight was pretty bomb, but aren't we going to learn about Jesus too?"

That hit me pretty hard and I almost got defensive, but I knew he was right. I even forgot to pray! It felt like we were throwing this huge party and having a blast, but completely forgot to invite the guest of honor! We do that in our faith a lot.

But my response to Landon felt more like a cover-up, as if that had been my plan all along. I said, "Oh yeah, we'll get there, I just wanted to hang with you guys tonight." It was blunt, with some truth, but honestly, more of a cop-out. I was reminded that night of what my purpose was there, and about the hearts and intellectual capacity of students and how nurturing them in the spirit of Christ was more important than just playing *American Gladiators*. It was up to me to get myself in line so I was at a point where I could offer that to these students and honor the God I loved and who had led me out to California. The ride home that night was one I'll never forget as everything hit me at once.

It was quiet. Probably too quiet in my jeep, as my ears were ringing from the silence. I usually used those times for calling friends and family to catch up or listening to music, but having any sort of sound that night did not appeal to me. I wasn't ready to go home, and I was at a point where something needed to change. Not just in my life, but in my heart. There was a desire and passion for something meaningful, lasting and beautiful. Before I knew it, I was pulled over in the high school parking lot. I'm not sure how I even got there, but the eight minutes it took to drive there felt more like an hour. I sat in the car for a few minutes. Now, looking back, I was feeling a connection with everything that night. The quietness of an almost eerie, fog covered campus, and the fact that I was so small and the things around me had grown so large were very evident. I started to get inspired.

I'm not sure it was all "legal" to be wandering around the campus that night, but it didn't occur to me in the moment and I didn't care. I hopped a fence and strolled around. There was a much different vibe from the day a few weeks prior when I had visited for lunch. I ended up sitting down on a bench with a few rows of green, semi-rusted out lockers in front of me. All the emotion I'd felt over the past month, the excitement, sorrow, questioning, everything came to a head and I realized that this entire move, my entire life had nothing to do with me. It's something that I've preached and spoken about a lot before, but for the first time I really understood it. In that moment I easily gave my life back to the God I loved so dearly, and along with that, I surrendered my time, thoughts, frustrations and triumphs.

There wasn't anything crazy. There was no sign that happened, no shooting star, just a broken person who finally realized that I couldn't do life on my own any longer. Even though I'd been teaching it for years, it never made sense until then. I didn't think of myself as a fraud however. I had been sincere. I prayed He would continue pursuing me and using me for His glory for the rest of my life.

The heavens didn't open up, nor did lightning strike from the sky. I was just a guy on a bench in the middle of the night who finally didn't feel alone in one of the most secluded environments I'd ever been in.

I stood up and starting a walking prayer. So often we think that prayer can only happen in a quiet corner of a bedroom, on our knees, hands folded with a Bible next to us on an end table with the lamp set to the dullest setting. I wanted my entire life to be a prayer! So many things came through in conversation that night. I prayed over my wife and my commitment to hold her up, I prayed over leadership and everything from the poor to world peace. Then I started standing in front of random lockers and praying that God would use these students in this community to change the world for His kingdom's glory. I felt there was going to be some kind of revolution of this current generation and that it was going to start in this small community in Southern California. My role became clear: To do anything I'm called and created to do. That sounds like such an easy task, right? But, after years of ministry and many years of learning about and struggling with my own faith, I was ready.

As I prayed that night on the school campus, a couple of images kept flashing in my mind. I had a pretty strong sense that I touched the locker of the student who told me "F---You," and the image of my own students and youth group kept flashing through my mind. What was going to happen at the church was going to be happening right on the ground that I was standing, on this very campus. The church isn't just the walls of the physical building; those were fragile in many ways, especially when tennis balls are involved. No, the church is the body of believers growing together and showing Christ wherever they are, and that was happening here and was going to start a fire throughout this place.

The few tears I shed that evening, and I'm not a crier, quickly turned from tears of disappointment and frustration, to tears of passion!

As I walked across the parking lot to my car, wondering how many calls and texts I missed from my wife curious about where the heck I was, I stopped dead in my tracks. I looked at my car from about twenty feet away and noticed something significant. No, it wasn't tee-peed and wrapped in saran wrap (that was a few weeks before as a "welcome" from the students), and no, it didn't have a flat tire. I realized it was parked in the exact same parking spot where I'd had the uncomfortable conversation with Tyler and his friends that last time I'd been there. The image was vivid as I flash backed to it. This parking lot probably held 500 cars, and mine was the only one parked there. For whatever that all meant, Tyler came into my mind, and I was a prayer warrior that night. I said a few words for him and got in to my jeep to drive the rest of the way home.

The first thing I did when I turned the car on was grab my ipod and I played "God of This City" by Chris Tomlin on repeat the rest of the way home, listening carefully to every word. "Greater things have yet to come, and greater things are still to be done in this city." That was so true.

4

U R THE CHURCH

"For even if the whole world believed in resurrection, little would change until we began to practice it. We can believe in CPR, but people will remain dead until someone breathes new life into them. And we can tell the world that there is life after death, but the world really seems to be wondering if there is life before death."
– Shane Claiborne, *The Irresistible Revolution: Living as an Ordinary Radical*

I couldn't sleep that night. I tossed and turned staring at the dark ceiling. I was feeling the impact of the emotions running through my system. This wasn't my plan for what was going to happen when I moved out here. I had been doing youth ministry for a lot of years, and at every church I served at, I swore it was the last time. To be completely honest, deep down my plan was to come to California to let my ministry die and ride off into the sunset. It's something you can't fake. It had always been a passion of mine, and I still genuinely loved students, but it wasn't all about playing games and entertaining. I wasn't a glorified baby-sitter. It's something you need to put your entire life and soul into. Most of the time people can read right through the "showiness" of it all. This is the true reason it made for such a tough transition job-wise. But at that point my heart was taking over my personal goals and selfish wants.

I entered the church the following day with a new perspective. I showed up quite a bit earlier than usual, and the adrenaline and emotion from the previous night hadn't worn off quite yet, so I was ready to do some work.

The other staff members were around and it was the morning of our weekly staff meeting. I showed up at the meeting with a little more optimism than I had had in previous weeks and meetings. We started out with a prayer and then on into the ever-so exciting details of our plan to change the world.

It's crazy to me the perception that many people have about working in a church. I've heard many times how "that would be the best place to work." As if somehow magically, there was no conflict, no lack of communication, always happy, loving people. But, I'd been there, I'd seen the great Oz behind the curtain, and it wasn't all glamorous.

The thing that made it hard was the constant pressure of needing to be "On" all the time. There was this sense that if you were on staff at a church and showed any vulnerability then it was tough for you to be a leader, because maybe you weren't in a strong enough place in your personal life to lead. Ironically, this is a huge contradiction to what the Bible says. That book is filled with broken people that were leaders too. The church is full of broken people, and I was hiding my personal brokenness in the depths of me away from the staff, afraid to bear my soul, or step out. I felt an unspoken judgment would follow and they'd see who I really was.

I'm not sure how much of that was in my head or actually true, but either way, I found it hard to open up and trust staff members for a variety of reasons. Which was quite difficult since I had such a relational job in the church, and it begged for an outlet of trust, accountability and love.

The staff meeting progressed, and as usual had gone on for about an hour and a half without any decisions being made about anything. As we sat around the oval shaped wooden table, many minor details were being discussed, as well as most people's opinion about everything that was irrelevant. I think that played into my calm, reserved nature joining that staff. I pretty much knew where people stood on many issues, and I didn't have the desire or energy to speak up with my own thoughts, since it seemed kind of pointless. Mostly I feared that the already long meeting would turn into many more minutes. Don't get me wrong, there was as much sincerity and real compassion as there were fake and inappropriate comments being made. That's how people are, even Christians, even people that work in a church—they're real.

The meeting was coming to an end and I had been doodling throughout our time on my calendar. Some if it was ideas and notes, but a lot of it was drawings of random things like farm animals and lighthouses. This was interesting because I never really drew much of anything. Those meetings brought out my creative side. At the finale of this meeting, I was anxiously awaiting my release so I could really start working on some planning, lessons and direction for the youth program. We closed in prayer and headed out. I was about two feet out the door when I heard the voice of our property manager. It was booming, almost startling. "Evan, do you got a minute?" he asked. I was thinking about something sarcastic, like "No, actually, I lost a few minutes during that meeting, but I will let you know when I get those back." But I didn't, and just said, "Yep."

He walked outside with me. He was an intimidating man, older bouncer-enforcer type. He asked me what exactly we were doing last night. I really didn't know what he was talking about, so it wasn't hard to play dumb. He asked again, with more interrogation. Then he said, "Who's going to pay for that window?"

Ah yes, the window! I had forgotten about that. "Oh yeah," I said, actually kind of relieved with a smile. "Not sure, we were playing a game of…" He stopped me and said, "How did YOU, let this happen?" very accusingly. "As far as I'm concerned, the youth shouldn't even be in the Sanctuary at all." Then walked away. I stood there for a moment thinking about the tone of his voice and words, and couldn't help but think about how much deeper that statement probably went. There have been many instances where something small, like that window, has happened, and people forget about the big picture. They forget to think about the lives that are being touched, the fun being had and relationships being built. It was truly a pet peeve of mine.

It seemed that sometimes people in the church were far more worried about a small window being broken, than the transformation of the life of a student. It was sad. I'm not all about breaking windows, but it was an accident. That kind of stuff happens sometimes as a direct result of ministry and working with kids. It was just too bad that it had to be the focus for someone. My focus was turned in another direction, I was ready to plan the next week's youth group, and the only thing I knew, was that I was pretty sure we'd probably need to steer clear of the sanctuary.

I was ready. It had been a week now since I'd seen the students. Since the night I had the revelation at school I was so eager for the students to start showing up. I had everything ready and in place by five. The students wouldn't come until at least seven. You say seven, so that means by 7:20 you can actually start. The students started showing up, a few could drive themselves, and the younger ones got dropped off. Then the younger ones would go over and want to hang with the older kids, as they played about nine different songs in ten minutes on their car stereos.

We started outside since it was still light out. For the first part of the evening we played a few games. Capture the Flag was a hit, and a few more mixers I had made up. Just as the kids were getting into it, and about a half hour after we started, I brought all eighteen of them inside to the youth room. They moaned and grumbled a little, but they went along with it, eager to see what we were going to do next.

All I had written on the board was "U R THE CHURCH." It was written in big, black letters in my not so flashy handwriting.

Most of the kids said it out loud when they walked in, with questions that I ignored. There are three things I've learned in my time of working with high school students as keys to building a relationship with them.

1. Earn the right to be heard by them, which can take some time.

2. Get to their level. I didn't say "down" to their level, which comes off as condescending, but find things they can relate to and don't force it by using stuff you've seen on MTV or something, they see right through that as not being natural and all credibility is lost.

3. Use self-deprecating humor. There is a place for confidence to gain some respect, but no one, especially a kid, wants to listen to someone they feel is arrogant.

So keeping those things in mind always, as soon as they settled down, I started in with my teaching by telling this story:

> *It was the spring of my freshman year of high school. It had been a pretty eventful year, and I was getting ready to become a sophomore. It was spring time and everyone was itching*

to get outside and be done with school. Even more so because it was Minnesota and we'd had such a brutal winter.

I was on my way to gym class, which I had sixth period in a seven period day. I was coming to class late, because I had a band lesson, which I would NEVER let on to anyone. I would have rather taken a tardy or gotten detention than tell my teacher in front of everyone that I had a band lesson. Anyway, I strolled into the locker room to find it empty. I guess I showed up a little later than I had thought I would. Our locker room was in what felt like the deepest, darkest dungeon of the school. You had to walk down a couple flights of stairs and down some old dark hallways to get there. And I won't ever forget that horrid stench once you hit a certain point. It was the cumulative B.O. from every student that graced that hallway daily, and there were many.

So I walked into an empty locker room and was a little confused at where everyone had gone because I didn't think we were going outside. I didn't see anyone in the weight room and I didn't hear any loud noises from upstairs in the gym. Then I noticed a sign on the gym teacher's office. All the sign said, was "NO DRESS, MEET IN THE GYM". Now again, I was a freshman, and pretty naïve. I was already carrying the anxiety of showing up to my favorite class late because I had come from a secret band lesson, so I was a little out of sorts and pretty anxious.

There were two teaching assistants in the office that were gracious enough to help me out though. Both of them were seniors, and both knew my brother since he was also a senior. So, fatefully, I asked them, "Hey, does this mean, NO Dress?" Because logically in my head, I thought that we might have to go up to the gym to have the nurse check us for scoliosis which had been done before, and we couldn't wear a shirt for that. Naturally, they looked at each other on cue, and said, "Yeah, strip down and head on up there." In my defense, yes, I thought it was weird, but what wasn't uncomfortable and weird in high school gym class, right? So, I stripped down to just my skivvies and started walking up this side staircase to the back doors of the gym.

I couldn't hear much because the doors were pretty heavy, but I did hear my teacher talking, so I kind of sneaked through the door. It made a louder creak than I thought it would, and before I knew it, in the blink of an eye, I was in the gym, standing in my unders. The door slammed behind me, courtesy of my two senior friends and I was staring my gym teacher and the guys in my gym class in the face. My teacher turned his head toward me and stopped speaking. The guys roared and I froze.

Now, a couple of things went through my mind at that time, and there are a couple things that you need to know to make this story better. The first was that at this time in my life, I hadn't quite "graduated" to boxers or boxer briefs, so yes, tighty-whities it was. And also, the jeers and laughter weren't just coming from the front of me, I was hearing surround sound. I turned to look at the entire girls' gym class sitting on the other side of the bleachers facing me. It turned out that we were up there for square dancing so we didn't need a uniform that day. Boy, did I get the wrong message!

At this point, the kids listening to me telling the story were just rolling. And I admit, it's pretty dang funny looking back, but that's when I hit them with some truth. I continued with this:

Yeah, it was pretty funny, embarrassing and awful at the same time. Those seconds felt like minutes. After I finally found a way out and back to the locker room, I dressed and headed back up. Trying to re-enter that room with a sense of confidence and pretending like none of it had happened.

I heard all of the jokes and snickering, but after class when I was about to leave school and never come back, someone came up to me and told me this, "Hey, I wanted to let you know that I've been laughed at a lot. I've been mocked, made fun of, spat at. I know exactly how you are feeling. I have been there before. But you are more important than other people's labels that they put on you."
That someone was Jesus.

It really was a turning point in my faith to

feel the love and embrace of the REAL Jesus
in my life during one of the hardest days I'd
been through. It showed me that Jesus wasn't
just on Sundays, He wasn't just at church,
and He wasn't just a guy that made me follow
a bunch of rules. He was involved in every
area of my life and there to lift me up. He was
a guy who was by my side in a high school
gym.
My prayer for you guys is that Jesus plays
that role in everything you do.

I went on to talk about the healing power that Jesus has and then pointed to the statement I'd written down on the board. "U R THE CHURCH." I told them things were going to happen in this community and at their schools, and it was going to be through them. They had the power to be Jesus. They could be that friend who says "I know how you feel."

One of the hardest things for me to hear is when people talk about the youth as being the "future of the church." That's bogus. If they believe they are the future, then what do they have to offer now? That statement makes them feel like they don't matter right now. I told them to NEVER let anyone tell them that they are the future, but to recognize their importance in the present.

I talked with a passion I hadn't felt in a long time, it was pouring from my soul. I tend to get fired up when I talk sometimes and tears of passion well up in my eyes. So much passion, and the students appeared ready and excited about their call to "Be The Church, right now."

Over the next few weeks, things started to happen around church and town. I basically turned my physical office into a virtual office at the local pizza place, Starbucks, the skate park and anywhere else where I'd run into kids. It's funny and a complete waste of money and resources to have a real office for a youth worker anyway. I was starting to establish more of what that looked like to our congregation. And of course, with any change or something new, there was questioning. I was feeling supported half of the time and the other half of the time had to defend questions about where I was and how I was spending my hours. As far as how I was spending my time, that was something that either people got, or they didn't. If it made sense that I was in the trenches with students and building relationships, then it was obvious. If it was something that needed to be explained in detail, well, then there were probably no combinations of words that would make sense to those people.

For the most part, none of it bothered me. Things were starting to happen. I'm much more of a results person than anything else. "If you build it, they will come" type stuff.

If there's something good happening (that goes for all walks of life, not just churches), people will find it. That was happening with the kids. I'd made contact with some local college students and young adults which resulted in a great group of young leaders excited about being part of something that was going on in the church youth group.

They cared much more about investing in the lives of students than just sitting around making sure kids weren't hurting each other or making out in the prayer chapel room.

During that time, there was an excitement that seemed to have been set in place long before any of us started uncovering it. It was a longing to reach out and dig deep, an outlet for creativity and experience giving and serving in a radical way.

The leadership team in place consisted of those few young adults and a couple talented, experienced youth worker veterans. Of the females, Amy was afraid of ketchup, but she could relate to students unlike most people I've watched try. It was a gift. She also knew almost as many movie quotes as I did, which was awesome and very impressive! We spoke mostly in movie quotes, which maybe is a form of tongues?

There was a married couple, Chad and Alexa. They were newlyweds, the lovey-dovey type, which high schoolers love to be around. Chad was about four times the size of Alexa though. He was a football guy with the most gentle heart and booming laugh to go along with his great smile and sense of humor. Alexa was tiny, with a huge heart. She loved working with high schoolers and bared her soul in such an open and honest way.

Megan was a leader of leaders. She had the most experience and life stories to share. She had the perfect personality and drive to really get into the kids' lives and world. She was the lead singer of the virtual youth leader band and quietly demanded respect from those around her. All of the leaders were very much loved. What wasn't there to like? Each one exhibited their own unique skills and talents. We had so many fun days visioning, joking and growing together.

There were a few other people that would plug in here and there. It was a program that was truly being built on the hearts of people that had been called to give of themselves for these students. There were no obligations or guilt trips, they truly wanted to be there for the students. Pure hearts of gold.

There was also Don and Bee, short for Beatrice, but we all called her Bee. Those were the youth ministry vets. They'd seen and done it all. They were the constant caretakers of the youth workers and supported everything in a major way. Similar to a Mommy and Daddy bear, nurturing their cubs, sharing a meal of porridge in the forest. OK, so that might be a little too much, but when was the last time someone you know ate porridge??

Everything was going really well. God was at work in the lives of dedicated people and students were feeling a sense of purpose in the direction their lives were headed. Nothing happens overnight, but during the whole process of deepening our faith and growing together, the table was set for a revolution and we were chowing down on the buffalo wings for hors d'oevers!

5

See You On The Field

"An ounce of practice is worth more than
tons of preaching."
– Mohandas Gandhi

That fall there was ministry happening. Not just in the form of Bible studies, but lives growing together. Mentoring, questions being raised, dodgeball being played, carpets being stained, prayers being prayed and life directions being sought.

There was one night in particular that was quite significant. Our leader, Megan, took out two high school boys, both on the wrestling team, in a pull-up contest. Another way was that I saw a video on youtube of a cow giving birth to a man, which I'll never forget as it haunts my thoughts still to this day. But besides that, we ended up having a very good discussion on what it means to reach out and how important it is for us as Christians to do that. We also talked about how it looks to do outreach and our personal role in reaching out to those we know and come in contact with. One image that sticks out from that conversation was picturing Jesus coming back on the Day of Judgment. He puts together two groups, you are in one group heading away with Him and your best friend is standing in the other. Now, picture yourself looking into your friend's eyes as they say to you, "Wait, you knew about this and you never told me?"

It's a message that needs to get out. It's the greatest story of love that's ever been told! I remember saying that if I can tell people how great I think the movie *The Goonies* is, then why can't I share about the story of my creator?

So yes, it was a great discussion, with many questions, opinions and comments that were all validated and thoroughly talked about. Yet that wasn't even the most impactful and meaningful part of the evening. After things were finished and everyone was gathering outside, I started locking up. I came around the corner into the parking lot and about wet my pants after a couple of excited freshmen decided to jump out of the large bushes at me. That never got old to them. They did it almost every week, to many different people, but the crazy thing was that you knew it was going to happen, yet it still startled you. Kind of like watching the same horror movie over and over and knowing when the killer will pop out but you find yourself still being surprised anyway.

I caught my breath, had a sarcastic laugh and shouted good night to Landon, who looked like he was leaving since he was lingering over by the road. Landon was a very bright kid, always friendly and the one who reminded me of my conviction to teach and not just play games. He was a peer magnet. Everyone seemed to be drawn to him because of his friendliness and humor. He also had compassion and wisdom far beyond his years; I picked up on that right away.

As he heard me, he turned to shout back, "Later, see you this week sometime." He usually stopped by to visit me when I was kicking it around the area at the mall or something. When I looked again, I noticed he wasn't alone but I couldn't recognize who was with him. For fear I'd leave that night, dwelling on the fact that I blatantly didn't say goodbye to a kid, who I'm sure would've balled himself to sleep that night in his pillow, I started a brisk jog over towards them. It was a little chilly, so I had my hands in my pockets as I barely picked my feet off the ground or bent my knees to get over there with a little urgency, so selfishly I could go home.

But, as I got up close, the face was familiar. It was Tyler! Now, it should be noted that he wasn't technically on the church grounds, it was a public sidewalk, but never-the-less there was no doubt that there was an intention by him to be around. He was calmer than the other times I'd seen him but seemed a little depressed or saddened, maybe it was just exhaustion. In any case, I said, "Hey, good to see you, you finally made it here." I didn't say it condemningly. There was no judgment and I think he fully picked up on my sarcastic, subtle humor and actually cracked a bit of a smile as he just stared at the ground.

I asked how he and Landon knew each other and Landon said, "Tyler and I grew up together."

Something I found out later was that Tyler had been more active in the church when he was younger. Something rubbed his parents the wrong way during an interim pastor's stay and they hadn't been back since. He'd grown away from the church and his parents had just recently started coming back, now that there was a new full-time pastor. Landon had always been a good friend to Tyler, even if it was just a "church" friend and not a school friend, which made sense, knowing Landon's social butterfly abilities.

We spoke as a trio for another couple of minutes, and the one most important thing I took away from that conversation, was that Tyler mentioned a soccer game that weekend. Apparently he was a soccer player, which was cool, because I had played all through college and beyond. I never mentioned that and since the nature of his comment wasn't directed toward me I let it go. But not really. I was already making a plan of attack in my mind. We said good night and I told him I'd see him at church again next week. We both smiled, knowing that wasn't about to happen.

When I got home, I gave JoHanna a hug and kiss. She had been watching *Sex and the City* reruns. It was sometimes tough coming home because she'd always be waiting for me eager to talk about the day, but I'd been talking all day and night and I was always ready to just relax, and not talk. So when I'd walk through the door, she'd shut the TV off, no matter what she was watching or where it was in the show so we could chat. However, the first thing I'd do is go to the computer to check e-mail or fantasy sports. I admit, very selfish on my part. Then JoHanna would huff and puff for a minute and I'd usually submit, reluctantly. We'd chat for a few minutes but always with the computer on my lap and fingertips ready to go when the conversation ended. It felt like waiting for the bell to ring during the last hour of the school day.

That night after I got back online, I checked my e-mail. It was always the work e-mail first, just to make sure nobody wanted anything from me or was looking for me. E-mail is evil and always has a way of making everything seem and sound so urgent.

It was all good though and I was in the clear. So the next thing I did was search for the high school boys' soccer team. I had played and coached soccer in the past so I was interested in that anyway, but my motive that night was different. I wanted to see the schedule so I could follow up with Tyler. It was a game of cat and mouse and since he had stepped on (or within a few feet of) my turf, the ball was in my court and I was ready to go into his world. Things at the church were going great, leaders were leading, kids were showing up and now I wanted to focus on an opportunity with this particular kid.

The following day, I left church around 2:00 p.m. I figured that would give me a little time to get over to the high school and find the soccer fields. I wanted to stake it all out before practice started, just so I didn't seem too out of place. How often do you know of someone who randomly goes to watch someone that they barely know at a sports practice? Not a game, practice. Yes, the Allen Iverson quote is blaring in my head, too. "We talkin' 'bout practice. Not a game, not a game, practice."

But it was true, it was just a practice and I know how bleak the crowds are at soccer games already, so I was sure I'd be noticed. I wanted to step into Tyler's world though. I eventually found the fields and parked nearby. To my surprise, the teams were already out practicing. It was all the soccer teams, boys and girls. All four of the fields were taken up and there was a sea of red and yellow pennies, which are the practice jerseys worn for training. I really didn't have any idea which field he'd be on, so I needed to ask someone. If I didn't, I would've really looked weird wandering from place to place, but if I had some direction, I could walk with more confidence and take my place as a spectator.

Thankfully I ran into this kid Connor, who was sitting on a curb reading a book. He was in my youth group and pretty quiet. He was sort of the opposite of most students I knew in that he was shy around church but at school apparently really opened up. I gave him props for that. He approached me and said, "Hey, what are you doing here?" That was always the typical question, which was awesome, because I loved answering it.

"I'm just here to hang out," I said, waiting for the naturally confused look back. But he just said, "Oh cool." I became confused then because he was a little too comfortable with it, especially considering how out of place and lost I looked walking near the sports fields. We talked about random stuff for a minute or two, I asked him how school was and he asked about the only thing he knew of me, church stuff. It's funny how students get the sense a lot of the time that since you work at a church, you must live at the church and do your laundry at the church etc. I could totally relate to that. I remember how weird it was to see old teachers from school shopping at the grocery store. It was crazy for me to see them out of the "school" setting, as I'm sure it was crazy to see me out of the "church" setting. I suppose that was something I was working on trying to teach when it came to faith, that church isn't about walls.

The last thing I asked him was if he knew what team Tyler was on and where they might be practicing. He pointed and said, "Yeah, I think he's on field three, right over there."

I said, "Thanks" and gave him the new cool handshake that all the kids were doing and that I'd been practicing for awhile. I managed to pull it off too, like it was NBD.

Connor left and I walked over by the field. There were about twenty guys on the team and a couple of coaches. They were doing warm-up drills, passing, trapping and all of that. I found a spot toward one of the goal posts. It was a pretty good spot because I was less noticeable there, but I could see and hear everything that was going on. It all felt good and comfortable to me. As I mentioned, I grew up on a soccer field and it had only been a few years since I had stopped playing. I missed it. Until that moment, I don't think I realized how much. I missed the smell of the grass and the comradery of the team. I even missed the practices and drills, which is something I would never have said at the time, and I probably just missed those because I wasn't doing them.

The team had circled up and the coaches gave directions. There were a few more drills and then it turned into a scrimmage. The time went by pretty fast and I guess my only agenda that day was to be noticed by Tyler. I was sure that he hadn't seen me yet. I thought that after practice I would catch up with him and say hey. One thing that was obvious to me during the practice was the team chemistry. They were well coached and all worked hard. And to my surprise, the loudest, most encouraging voice on the field was Tyler. He was always vocal, constructively criticizing, while at the same time picking his teammates up and being an encourager. A far cry from the person I had painted him to be. Maybe the soccer field just changed that in him, or maybe he was a natural born leader and encourager. I smiled watching the potential that this kid had and kept thinking about what it would be like if He was to use those gifts and skills in every area of his life, including his faith.

Practice was over and I continued to linger. It had gotten less intense at this point, so I think I was noticed a little bit more by the team. The coaches had glanced at me a few times, I'm sure mumbling to each other, "What the heck is that guy doing here?" and wondering if they'd have to call campus security. But it was all good. There was a ball near the sideline where I was standing, so I picked it up and started making my way over to Tyler. This was another "out of my comfort zone" experience, but it's what I have always felt is important to do. If I was going to break down walls, build relationships and grow myself as well, I needed to have those experiences.

I kind of nodded to the coaches, who were a little less threatened. They were about my age and there was sort of an unspoken, "it's cool," between us. I walked up to Tyler and a couple of his teammates, in a non-threatening manner. The teammates happened to be his friends, Luke and Pete that he'd been smoking with a few weeks before when I saw him at school. They both were about the same size and built like stocky athletes. Teams kind of travel in packs, and I kept wondering how the heck they were smokers, but could run for two hours straight at practice. Anyway, as I got close Tyler saw me and his body language told me that it wasn't a surprise, so I'm sure he'd seen me already.

I walked up confidently and said, "Hey good practice, you guys looked good out there." I wanted to just move right past the uncomfortableness. When you're out there in your element on the field though, relating on sports or something, it all tends to make a little more sense and they were surprisingly responsive. We made a little small talk, and when I sensed that it had gotten awkward enough, I pulled out the ace up my sleeve. I hadn't done it in years but figured I'd see if I had anything left in the tank. I dropped the soccer ball that I was still holding and started juggling. I pulled off the shoulder to shoulder juggle and the around the world. I had been a pretty good player. The guys and coaches had all turned their heads at this point, if in anything, just some respect. I was so thankful that I didn't botch that. When I thought I had enough positive attention, I popped the ball up in the air and on its way down, ripped a one-timer from about twenty-five yards out, toward the goal. I hit it hard and buried it in the upper right corner inside of the post by about a foot. I couldn't have done that again if I had 100 more tries...

I heard a couple of oohs and aahs, and a "who is that?" But most importantly I felt the sense of breaking through a wall with Tyler and a couple of his friends. They lit up a little and started asking me how long I played and all that. I really didn't talk about it much. It wasn't about me, I was just stoked that they were genuinely interested, even if at first it was only about my soccer skills.

"Hey, that's pretty tight, but I could've made the shot," Tyler said jokingly, with a hint of arrogance. They all kind of laughed and I smiled. It was innocent banter, which was something else I missed about being on a team. I sensed a little competition coming on, so I said, "Prove it." He then put his cleats back on, grabbed his ball and got ready to shoot. Everyone there had now gathered, even the ones that had started walking to the locker room already. Tyler popped the ball up and struck it well-right of the goal.

"Damn!" he said. I looked at him and the crowd that was now gathered and said, "Yep, I guess I was a little closer." They all laughed, mocking him some, but definitely had the back of their leader over this random dude in street clothes that showed up. The one coach came up to me, Coach O'Brien, and asked my name. I told him and we talked for just a minute. He turned out to be a nice guy and then asked me if I'd ever considered coaching. I told him I had coaching and playing experience and how I had just moved to the area and would be available if he ever needed anyone to help volunteer a couple times a week. He told me he could always use quality help, especially volunteer, and that I should call him the next day. He gave me his number and then headed out.

That was a good day, but the best part came right after that as I turned back around to the group of guys, who now officially had broken for the locker room. The only ones left were Luke and Pete, waiting for Tyler to pick his stuff up. I walked back over to them and as Tyler stood up, I asked him if he was fast. "Huh?" he said. "I'm just curious if you're fast at all," I said. "What do you mean?" he asked again. "Like, could you beat me in a race over to that ball you kicked?" The ball that had finally stopped rolling across the blacktop onto the basketball court.

He understood what I meant, and again, as high school kids always wanted to compete and prove themselves we took off running! We both sprinted, but he looked like Usain Bolt against the out of shape twenty-nine-year-old that I was. Once we got over to the ball I said, with what little breath I had left, "Dang, you part cheetah?..." We laughed together and had a good walk and quick talk back over to the guys. I told him that the coach had invited me to help out. And to my surprise, he said, "That'd be cool." It was an in. It was an invitation to become a part of his life. At least that's what it felt like to me. A kid that was rough around the edges, with a foul mouth and some obvious God-given gifts and talents had now invited me in. I couldn't wait to learn more about this kid. He reminded me a lot of myself when I was his age.

I said goodbye to Tyler, Luke, and Pete and started heading off the field. I said a prayer during that walk and told God to use me however he wanted, then I said a prayer for those three guys.

After I left the field, I felt a good sense of accomplishment and commitment, that in some form, ministry had happened on that soccer field with those guys. That was outreach, going into the land of high school kids and getting into their lives with a genuine interest.

—⁓—

I got back to church; I had only been gone for about an hour or so, but I had forgotten to tell the office where I was. Apparently the Senior Pastor was looking for me and I was gone, so I had a message from him on my answering machine. He wanted to talk to me.

I went straight into his office, and while I wasn't scolded, I did feel a sense of questioning in his voice.

"Where did you go?" he asked.

"Oh, I was just up at the high school, I checked out soccer practice."

"Did you tell anyone you were leaving?" he asked.

"No, I guess I totally forgot." All the while thinking that I'd been gone about an hour and I'm sure the world didn't erupt while I was away.

He then said, "Well, that is why I was looking for you anyway. There has been some concern about where you are and how you are spending your time. I just want to make sure that we're keeping you accountable."

Now, I usually get defensive by nature, but I had been working on that. At this point, I was more discouraged and saddened by what he was saying.

"We want this to work out," he continued, "and we want to support you and have your back with things. That's why it is important that we know where you're at." This time, trying to come at it a little lighter, like we were on the same team.

Unfortunately, at this point I hadn't built any trust up with him yet either. I was building great friendships with many amazing people at the church, but not really with him. It was difficult to do. It had always seemed to me that he would've been amazing at managing a fortune 500 company with the skills he had, but when you're a pastor of a church and you seemingly lack compassion and show arrogance, it's hard to be mentored by that person. I sat in the chair, feeling like I was in the principal's office. I'm sure building it up in my head to be way worse of a situation than it actually was, but it felt like such a buzz kill.

I wanted to tell him about what I'd been doing, how I could see God at work on the local high school campus, within our ministry team, and even in myself. But I felt as though I'd mentioned that plenty in the past and it was all being overlooked. Most of the time I would only be called into meetings to be "corrected," and never to be built up with any sort of praise or encouragement. I believe both are needed, when done appropriately.

My response was more than lackluster as I felt the wind from the sails of the soccer field die down in an instant. "No, I get it. I'm sorry. I'll work harder at it," I said with much more defeat than optimism.

"OK," he said. "I really want you to succeed here," he reiterated again. I couldn't help but wonder if that statement shouldn't have been followed by "for my own sake." Or if it implied that I wasn't succeeding already and there was still a little hope of that. In any respect, I was starting to feel a sense of defeat, mere minutes after a sense of hope and triumph on the soccer field. I spent the rest of the day sitting at my desk, fake reading, while really just thinking about what I needed personally at that time. It was time for this E.T. to phone home. I needed to seek out some encouragement for myself, since the place I should've been getting it from, I wasn't.

6

Filling My Funnel

"Material possessions, winning scores, and great reputations are meaningless in the eyes of the Lord, because He knows what we really are and that is all that matters."
– John Wooden

We're all built like funnels. No matter what we do in life we all need to be filled and fueled. There's so much going out the bottom of us, wait, does that sound weird? But honestly, there are many demands of our time, energy, talents and commitments and if we're constantly pouring out, we'll eventually run out of whatever we have to offer. I think there is a reason why funnels are so much larger on the side where the initial pour comes in, it's because we need to be filled up first in order to give. I've always said that good intentions will give you a cup, but good actions will fill it. The funnel is along the same lines, there's a need we all have to be filled and poured into, and once we receive that, we are able to give. Just talking about it doesn't work; we need to be doing.

Working in a position where you are constantly giving can really drain you fast if there isn't anything coming in. This is the case for many in ministry and the danger is not recognizing or acknowledging it before it's too late. That's why the turnover in many youth positions is frequent.

But, I had learned from my past, I understood what I needed and the warning signs which told me when I needed refueling.

I called a few people that evening. A couple of them were close friends from high school and college who knew me so well that it didn't matter how long it'd been since we'd last talked, or where we were at in life, it still felt comfortable. Those kinds of people are hard to find. I could call them anytime for a vent session or to be reminded of where I'd come from.

I also called my old youth pastor from high school, Mark. He always seemed to have the right words and timing. He had somehow mastered the art of dealing with people and it showed from his example of putting together a lengthy youth ministry career. Mark was a guy that looked as though he had it all together and figured out, yet yielded a distinct openness of being real and authentic which drew people in to him. Nobody wants to feel vulnerable and broken around someone they feel can't relate and who seems perfect. That was part of my experience growing up, thinking everyone in my church was perfect and wondering how

I would fit in, when I felt so screwed up compared to them. There are a lot of "C" words that are intimidating about the Christian faith: Christ, Commitment, Church, Christianity etc…, but I think one of the toughest is Compare.

Mark listened with the same sincerity as always. I shared with him about my homesickness, my struggles, my frustrations, but also my call and vision for how God was using me in the position I was in. Then he said some encouraging words that he was so good at speaking, "Evan, when someone says something to you, whether good or bad, I'm convinced that it's 25 percent about you, and 75 percent about them." That took me some time to digest but it became a way that I would view situations so I wouldn't get as frustrated or down on myself, but also to not give myself a big head when I'd receive praise. He also talked to me about working with different people and said that "people are people, whether in a church or not." Something I'd been really experiencing lately. No matter how long or short the conversations with Mark were, it always ended with my funnel being overflowed and I was refueled again.

Sunday came that week before I knew it. I always had mixed feelings about Sunday mornings; I guess based mostly on what my role in the services were and what my agenda was that day. I was learning and seeing that there really were some great and amazing people at the church and good community happening. I'd get heartfelt bear hugs from some of the old ladies and have supportive conversations with parents of the students. If there was ever a time working in a church that you needed to put your game face on, it was Sunday morning!

It was a typical Sunday as everything went decently smooth. A greeter didn't show up, so they grabbed a random guy in the back row who was just visiting to help do it. Also, the power point was just a little off, which wasn't a huge deal, except when the pastor was doing announcements and was relying on the screen for those as well as the prayer he was going to read to the congregation. All things the average church-goer probably didn't even notice or care about but is more apparent when you work there. The music was good as usual though. I've always thought that if there were better musicians playing together on a Sunday morning somewhere, it'd probably have to be in heaven.

I was leaving the church patio after the last service to go back and lock the doors near the youth wing, when I saw Tyler standing back by the main sanctuary doors. He'd come to church that morning with his parents. I couldn't help but wonder if it was because I'd been to practice that week, but either way, I darted over to him. This was a different element for him, not his comfort zone and he was still trying to figure me out, as I was him. Luckily, his parents were talking with a few other people so it allowed me to get a few minutes of conversation with him.

I asked him, "What'd you think of the sermon?" He kind of shrugged and said, "They are all the same, whatever." I got the impression that he probably didn't listen to much of it, and I'll admit, I didn't really either that day, but I wanted get his attention, so I said, "Wasn't it cool when he was talking about the time he rode the elevator with Michael Jordan and then tripped him by accident after they walked out, and MJ twisted his ankle and couldn't play in the all-star game that year?!"

His face lit up a little and he cracked a smile as he asked with a lot of interest, "What? Are you serious?"

Feeling good that I'd cracked his facade, I said, "Nope. Not at all. I just wanted to make sure you weren't listening to the sermon."

But then he went cold as he said very matter of factly, "Look, it's all the same. I've been going to church since I was young, I get it. I know all about Christianity and about God. I just think all organized religion is stupid."

So, I asked back, "Okay, so based on that belief, how are you choosing to live your life?" I wasn't trying to be condemning, just curious and wanted to make him think a little.

He said, "What? What do you mean? None of that matters until you die anyway, and if there is a God I'll probably go to heaven, my parents are praying for me."

I want to make one thing clear, I would never say who will or won't go to heaven, I'm not God and I don't get to judge that. Thank God! I would never want that responsibility. But I do know that God has a plan for each one of us and that He's created us for a specific purpose. My own joy and purpose in life was to see others realize that in their lives and enter into the abundance of life that God has called us to! Nothing was more exciting to see and nothing feels better than when we're living how we were intended, and that was to glorify God and surrender our lives to His service and will. Much like the purpose of a baseball bat is to play a game of baseball and hit the ball. If used for something else, it loses its significance and could even be used in a negative way and become destructive and unfulfilling. That goes for pretty much anything that was created for a specific purpose. So how much more complicated and meaningful is a human life? I thought that was relevant here and was thinking that through while talking with Tyler.

I then said, "Hey man, I respect your thoughts. I'd like to hear more about it." I meant it, too.

"Yeah, well we gotta go," he said as he turned to walk away.

"No, that's cool, I meant sometime soon. You want to come to youth group this week? We're playing human Mario-kart in the parking lot (which is the best game ever) and doing a study on the Gospels."

He quickly tried to make up an excuse by saying, "No, I have something going on." But it actually just meant he wasn't interested.

Thankfully my next question was, "Do you like buffalo wings?"

"For sure," he said.

"Great dude, after practice sometime this week, I'll take you out for some wings."

"That'd be cool," he said while nodding.

"Right on, let's plan on it. Have a great rest of your day!" And I left.

As I walked away, I was just thinking about what the contrast would've been if I had said, let's go to the church office this week and talk, as opposed to, let's go to the mall for some buffalo wings. Context means everything when it comes to how things are viewed, especially the threat level of the unknown.

—ᴍ—

I had officially accepted the opportunity to be an assistant coach for the boys' varsity soccer team. My commitment would be light but still significant. It was a volunteer position but gave me a good outlet. It ended up being an easier sell to the church than I first thought because of its potential to connect with students and the school. And that next Wednesday after practice, I took Tyler out for buffalo wings, just as we'd talked about.

Again, context is huge. That's why I have always been conscious about my surroundings as far as hanging out with people. It's a psychological thing and there's a difference between chatting with a student at school, at church or in a public restaurant, and this time it was all neutral ground. Tyler was standing in the school parking lot near his car, texting on his phone when I picked him up. We made small talk driving and walking through the mall. We chatted about the soccer team and then about what stores we liked to shop at. I even brought Tyler into the Apple store to give me his opinion on a computer that I had no intention of ever buying. But it was cool to see how much he knew about it and get his input.

We got to the restaurant. It was a little hole-in-the-wall BBQ place tucked into the corner of the mall. It wasn't the food court area and it was still early, so there weren't many people inside. I told Tyler to order anything he wanted, which ended up being a full plate of wings, the same as me. The conversation still remained low-key at that point. We talked about our threshold of hotness when it came to wings and spicy foods. I told him about a guy I knew in college that ate ten wings at a local joint, and the sauce on them was called "Devil's Spit." And I quickly shared how later that night he was rushed to the emergency room because he'd burned a hole in his esophagus! True story, but he survived.

Naturally the conversation progressed into family, church and all of those more personal things. Although Tyler had a confidence about him, he was definitely guarded when it came to freely offering up that type of information. I understood it, but was curious about what hurt and pain were behind that reluctance.

We eventually got to talking about the youth group.

I asked, "So, do you have any friends in the youth group?"

He answered, almost mockingly back, "No," as he smirked and arrogantly chuckled.

"Do you know a lot of the kids?"

"Yeah, but most of them are annoying, they just aren't my kind of people."

I was slightly offended by that, only because I really liked the students that I'd been working with and genuinely thought they were pretty great kids.

But, I had a heart for Tyler too, and shrugged it off to his tough exterior.

Of course, my next question then was, "Tell me who 'your kind of people' are."

"Just like people who like to have a good time, not churchy," he said, saying it as if "churchy" people couldn't have a good time.

"And those types of people aren't in the church?"

"Nope, church people are all hypocrites and judgmental."

I've known so many wonderfully real, authentic and humble people within the church, but I also understood exactly where he was coming from. And sadly that's an opinion carried by so many in the world. It's too bad that a small percentage of people are the ones that can make the most noise and seem to set that tone.

I affirmed his thought. I said, "Yeah, I can see how you could say that and it's around for sure. I just don't think that it's *all* church people. I also think if that's what people see when they view the church, they are really missing the point."

He looked at me as if he didn't care, but also had a slight glimmer of trying to process what else the church could be. We conversed for a few more minutes about the topic. It was a good conversation. There was nothing heated and I could feel there was a vague sense of trust he was starting to form with me and so he shared a few more things about his image of church, his experience with church and his view of God. Some of it broke my heart to hear, but I was just looking to try and understand where this kid was coming from. I appreciated his openness.

I didn't speak a whole lot and it got to a point where he had talked almost too much about it in his own mind, where he finally caught himself and quickly changed the subject back to soccer. We didn't re-visit any of the "religious" talk.

As I dropped him off after dinner, I told him that it'd be really cool for him to try out a youth group sometime soon. He mumbled something like "maybe sometime," and got into his car in the school parking lot. He was the most interested, "non-interested" kid I'd probably ever met.

After I left, I went back to my office to pick up a few things, check my voicemail and then headed home. When I got inside I saw JoHanna lying on the couch watching TV, but the sound was turned low. She didn't look up or even lift her head, and I could tell that she hadn't been sleeping. It looked like she was just staring blankly at the TV and her eyes looked puffy. Cautiously I asked her what was up, and did so with my "everything's always good" optimistic tone. She barely offered a head shake. Something was clearly not all right, but I couldn't figure out what was wrong. Selfishly, I would always assume it was about me, and then also try to fix it right away.

I started asking over and over, which I'm sure was getting extremely annoying. "What's wrong? Huh? Tell me." Followed by, "What did I do?" "I didn't do anything," immediately getting defensive. As soon as I said that, she said, "Yep, you're right." Then she hopped up, grabbed her glasses and went into the bedroom and shut the door. Before I could follow her into the bedroom I glanced at the floor next to the couch where she had been laying. I saw a crumpled up box and used Kleenex. My heart sank into my stomach. At that moment I understood and anticipated the upcoming conversation. All of the selfishness I'd shown and had in me turned to sorrow. Could it have been that I was so wrapped up in the lives of others that I had neglected my own wife? The one person in my life that deserved the most attention and who I was supposed to grow with was empty and alone.

I walked into the bedroom to see her sitting with her back to the door leaning over crying. It was an image I never wanted to see, but can't shake from my memory. I sat behind her without knowing what to say. I could always fix things and I had always been able to talk things through, but my neglect of the love and respect for my wife had taken a back seat to my job and personal agenda. I questioned what God was doing in my life and got frustrated and angry at Him and myself for not loving my wife how I should've, not having enough hours in a day, and for allowing things to get to that point.

We talked that night. We talked a lot. I never had a feeling that it was being repaired as we talked, but I had a renewed sense of family that I needed to make a priority again. She shared how she hardly had any faith, and that it was so difficult to watch me come home having been submersed in it all day, talking about what God was doing in the lives of students and sharing brief snippets of what I was teaching on, and how cool it was. Yet I was never letting her in on any of it. It was one of the biggest reasons she married me and I realized I needed to start being the spiritual leader for the family.

I thought I was being obedient. I thought I was doing God's work. I could see results and fruits and all of that, but I was not being the husband I needed to be. Except for my relationship with God, my marriage was most important. This wasn't a quick fix, this wasn't even a promise for the future; I had already made that within our wedding vows. This was a time when I needed to put my money where my mouth was, not be selfish and include my wife. She told me she was proud of me, that she loved what I was doing and could see my heart over-flowing, but didn't like that she wasn't involved in any way. All she wanted was to be a part of it all, be a part of my life, and for the past few months, she hadn't even felt noticed. That's the part that probably affected me the most. She didn't want to be a part of youth group, she wanted to be a part of me, and deep down, that's what I wanted and needed too.

That was a long night; a side of ministry people rarely see. I was often asked why my wife wasn't at church. To anyone on the inside, they should've known and seen it. All she wanted was an opportunity to grow and worship with her husband, and since she wasn't getting that at home when we were alone, why would she ever think that coming to a church activity where I was busy the entire time chatting, teaching and leading that she'd ever get a second of my time or a chance to grow with me? My ever-changing life got rocked that night, and my perspective changed for the good.

Over the following days I needed to make things right or at least start on the path to making it good. If things weren't good at home, then nothing in life was going to be good, that was just a fact, but never in my life was there another time when that was so apparent. I also realized that it wasn't just the growing spiritually together part that was missing; it was just simply showing my wife love and care in general. So, I took the following day off from work. I used it so I could figure some things out and get my priorities straight. Not only had I not been a good husband, I had also neglected myself. As much of an extrovert as I am, the way I got my energy was time alone, not surrounded by others. I'm sure that would surprise a lot of people, but it was true. I was becoming a work-a-holic and in life, especially the church, that was a very big problem. "Being busy" is something that addicts a lot of people, and I had fallen victim to it. There's a distinct difference between being a hard worker and being a work-a-holic.

This time however, it came down to me and my responsibility. This was bigger than just a vent session with old friends or a mentor, this was real and I did a lot of soul-searching during that time. That particular day off was spent buying a care package for my wife. I put a lot of thought and energy into getting every little treat, snack or gift that would make her smile and show her appreciation. I know that money and presents don't make it all good, but it was a start. I knew that my presence meant more than my presents by far. I also wrote her a poem and a letter. It was deeply heartfelt and rekindled the flame that I never noticed was flickering in my heart.

I also bought us a book of love devotions and we started attending a new mega church together on Saturday nights. It was something that we had always talked about, but hadn't followed through on, which was mostly my fault. We loved the pastor and it became like a date night. Things were getting better and we were so much in love. The truth was that it was like we were on opposite sides of a triangle and at the top point was God. The closer we got to God on a personal level, the closer we came together to the point where God was on the tip of the triangle, as one in our relationship.

I had been at my church and lived in California all of three months and my life had been completely turned upside down and back again in so many ways. It was a roller-coaster of teaching and learning, loving and struggling, questioning and growing, and I would not have traded it for anything else. Those are the ways we grow. When we're faced with trials and adversities, it's amazing to see the people that we become, and that's what God is interested in as well!

7

Gaining Momentum

"It's crazy, if you think about it. The God of the
universe-the Creator of nitrogen and pine needles,
galaxies and E-minor loves us with a radical,
unconditional, self-sacrificing love. And what is our
typical response? We go to church, sing songs and
try not to cuss."
– Francis Chan, *Crazy Love*

The youth group at church continued to go smoothly and grow as kids began inviting their friends. Not just because it was fun either, but because God was moving in their lives and they wanted to share it with others. It was really starting to become something special. Spirits and numbers were up and we were in a good groove with the school year. It was November, so I think everyone was getting excited for the holiday season stuff, but what I was getting ready for was camp! We were heading to winter camp up in the mountains in a few weeks and had started sign-ups. I was excited and pretty curious to see what this camp would be like. The kids talked about it all of the time, so in some ways I felt like I'd already been there. There is something powerful about the camp experience and it's what a lot of youth programs will focus their year around as being the most pivotal and important event. It's about getting away from your normal routine to be intentional about listening and learning outside of your home environment. Another element of the camp experience is bonding in the close quarters of the cabins!

With all of that in mind, I had a goal of bringing up as many kids as possible. We had a bus rented and it fit thirty students comfortably, but my goal was to make them get us another bus! So we were promoting camp heavily, and even offering scholarships at youth group. One night word got around school and the kids were buzzing that we were going to give away two full camp scholarships that night at youth group. It was the biggest group of students I had seen so far, a pretty awesome sight. Even though I knew a lot of them were only there because they wanted to go to camp, and they did nothing else the rest of the year. Some of their motives I'm sure weren't necessarily to grow deeper in faith, but probably to try and hook up with the guy or girl they liked, or maybe just to get away from their parents for a long weekend. Either way, it was cool to have so many students show up. I'd rather see every kid I could up at camp, no matter what their reasoning was, because I knew what a lot of the alternatives were for a high school kid on the weekends and I also knew God had control of their hearts, not me.

For the record, that night a guy named Devin and his girlfriend Rachel won the two scholarships. They stood for an hour and a half with Rachel on Devin's back and her feet never touching the floor, while Devin withstood all the pain. Props to them, they were cool kids.

I was continuing to coach soccer as the season was winding down, and not surprisingly I hadn't seen Tyler anywhere else but the soccer field. During that time I was getting to know the other kids on the team pretty well too. That included Tyler's good friends Luke and Pete. I could hold my own with them and they were a fun group to be around. They would try to push my buttons and get a rise out of me, but they'd always get frustrated when they saw that they couldn't. Most of them were a little rough around the edges, which I liked, but I could read right through them. I knew they had good hearts somewhere beneath all of the F-bombs and negative talk about girls. I embraced my opportunity to be a role model for them. It was a public school, so of course I couldn't talk about the Bible, faith or anything like that, but that wasn't really why I was doing it anyway. There were a lot of kids that didn't have solid male role models and I felt I could give them my best attempt at being one.

They all knew I was a Youth Pastor, and I'd hear crap for it, but that was always sweet because if they asked questions, I could answer them! Being able to answer their questions was the silver lining for having to stay mum about Bible talk. I will admit however, that I blurred those lines a little bit at times.

After practice one day that week, I just straight up asked Tyler, Luke, and Pete if they wanted to go to camp with us. Now, they didn't respond exactly how I thought, meaning laughing it off and saying some inappropriate thing comparing it to band camp or something, but they also didn't say yes. There was thought, at least a slight interest in what camp was and where. That was my chance to build it up. I told them it was in a really bomb location up in the mountains, had rock-climbing walls, snow for snowball fights and the girl/guy ratio at present was 2/1 in our group. I knew the real selling points for those guys. Even though it pained me to have to go visit snow again, since that was a big reason we'd moved away from Minnesota in the first place, I had to remember that these kids never got to see it, so even the smallest amount was a huge deal to them! They had no idea about the evils of a five month winter filled with snow and ice.

Ultimately they all tried to make excuses, but a few minutes later after Luke and Pete took off, I pulled Tyler aside. I told him that I really wanted him to go to camp with our group. At this point, we'd spent some time getting to know each other and he at least acted as though he'd give it some thought. I shared with him the deeper side of camp and about the camp speaker and how it wouldn't be like the sermons at church, that it was totally geared toward high schoolers. He was reluctant, but didn't quite shut the door on it. As I mentioned before, this kid was serious and there was something brewing in him that maybe camp would help him deal with.

A couple weeks had passed and we were only one week away from loading the bus to camp. We were actually pretty close to the fifty I had hoped for, and knowing how kids and parents are with signing up at the last second, I knew we were in good shape. So the second bus was ordered! There was also a solid group of adult leaders going. They were our steady leaders and mentors, Chad and Alexa, Amy, Megan, and a few more that just wanted to help for the weekend. I don't like the word "chaperone." I never have, but especially in youth ministry when you're looking for adults that want to work with students. To me, when I hear the word chaperone, I picture someone standing against the wall at a middle school dance, only leaving their post to make sure no one is dancing too close with someone of the opposite sex. We didn't need chaperones, we needed adults who really wanted to invest in the lives of students, all students, not just the ones they related to best. And with any adult leader or sponsor, they needed to have the natural gift of grace. Trust me, for anyone that's ever worked with students, and especially gone on an overnighter with them, grace was very much a necessity.

Only a couple nights before we left for camp I decided to give Tyler one more try. He continued to be on my heart but had also continued to be wishy-washy in his decision making when it came to going up to camp. Although he never actually said no, I knew where he was. Soccer had ended that last week, so I knew he was going to have some down time. We had gotten closer through soccer, close enough to where he had given me his cell phone number. Here is the text conversation from that night:

DUDE, GOT 1 MORE SPOT FOR CAMP W UR NAME ON IT
Sry, can't go
U SURE, IT'S GUNNA BE BOMB.COM
Haha, nah, just don't kno anyone and no $ thx tho
WHAT IF I PRMSE IT'LL BE THE BEST WKND OF UR LIFE?
How? Doubt it.
JUST THINK ITLL B WORTH IT
Prob a waste of time. Hav fun

At this point, I could've just given up, but at the risk of straining the relationship some and getting annoying, I tried one more desperate plea:

IF U GO AND DON'T HV FUN, I WILL PAY UR WAY!
Really? And u'll stop asking me to come to church stuff?
SURE. IF U GO, I'LL LEAVE U ALONE ABOUT YG STUFF. DEAL?
PLUS, I NEED U ON MY TEAM FOR SNO FTBALL
OK deal. I'll go. Just to prv how lame it is.
AWS! BEST DECISION OF UR LIFE!

I was amazed! I still don't know what got to him; the guilt, my annoying persistence, the boredom he saw staying at home, the chance to get away from his parents or the deeper longing he felt for something significant. I'd like to think it was God working in his heart. But for whatever reason, Tyler was coming with us to camp!

8

The Camp Experience

"Christ is the strongest, grandest, most attractive personality ever to grace the earth, but a careless messenger with the wrong approach can reduce all this magnificence to the level of boredom... it is a crime to bore anyone with the Gospel."
– Jim Rayburn, Founder of Young Life

We met at the buses that Friday at noon. There was a lot of chaos and excitement as all of the parents and students pulled into the parking lot to start loading and getting ready to leave. Much of the excitement was built around the buzz of camp, a lot of it had to do with having a large group around, and on top of that the kids got let out of school early that day which alone jumbled up their routine. Many of them had already been together for a good part of the day, even the night before since many parents let their kids miss the entire day of school. It was something with the school district where they had to have so many school hours within the given year. They'd make them go for a half-day here and there to compensate instead of just a full day off, so really there wasn't much happening in classes on those particular days anyway, therefore it was not a big deal for the kids to miss. They also all had Monday off, which was part of the reason the camp worked so well for us because it was a full three nights and a little longer than a typical weekend.

As students arrived we had some of our key parents and volunteers helping to check them all in, so naturally they were running up to me and asking "Who's this person?" "Who's that?" There were a lot of new kids coming with us, some that I hadn't even met yet, which made it a little tough. But those weren't the only questions I was getting from every angle; When do we leave? When are we getting home? What do I need to pack etc.? As if all of this information had not been readily available for weeks and in many different capacities: website, postcards, mailers and verbal announcements just to name a few. That got old, especially when I would have to be sincere and respect the students and parents as if I hadn't been hearing the same questions over and over. The one about "Do I need this?" always got to me because I'm standing there looking at them, the bus and their luggage, thinking "Does it matter now? We're leaving in like fifteen minutes…"

I was personally anxious and had my own bit of excitement and fear going on inside. I had been to many camps and had many overnighters with students, but this was my first with this group, so I wasn't sure if there would be some that turned wild and crazy at the stroke of midnight or something, like a Gremlin. I had been having nightmares the week leading up to camp that I would be waking up some morning tied to a tree outside of our cabin wearing just my blue and red boxer briefs with lipstick and chocolate drawings all over me. But don't worry, that didn't end up happening.

I was also getting anxious because I was staring through people as they talked to me while I kept my eyes open for Tyler. He had promised me he'd come and try the camp thing out and I hadn't seen him yet. It was well past noon and we had most of the group there and ready to go, so I had a few people help me corral the entire crew of parents and students together to make one huge circle. This took a little time to do, but we really weren't in too much of a hurry. In my head the goal was to leave by one, so we still had plenty of time to make that work, hence the noon departure time that was told to everyone.

As we finally got everyone into a circle I saw Tyler pull up and park a little further down the parking lot from everyone else. He hopped out of his car carrying just a backpack and I figured he was going to come and tell me that he wasn't going. I started feeling a little bummed, but at least he'd showed up to tell me. However, I had just gotten everyone's attention so I needed to make my announcements before I talked to him. I gave a quick overview of the trip, AGAIN, to everyone this time, told them when we were looking to get home and also expressed excitement for what I felt God was going to do over the next few days. We had the pastor pray over our group and then I said one last thing. I reminded everyone, in a very appropriate way, that drugs and alcohol weren't welcome on the trip and if that was the plan for some of the students to sneak it along, they'd be sent home immediately and parents would be called. Our students were generally really good, but I also knew some of the potential decisions they could make, and since many of them were new, to be fair I gave them an out right up front.

I told them, "If this is your plan, I've set up a garbage can in the far corner of the youth room and within the next few minutes before we leave you can go over and toss out whatever poor decisions are in front of you, no questions asked." This wasn't to condone it, but also not condemn it. If you want to do youth ministry, a huge key is to meet students where they're at, and if that's where they were at, you just needed to be real about it and get to the deeper issues of their lives first before working on their lifestyle choices.

The next few minutes were spent giving hugs, saying goodbyes and heading off to the bathroom. The bathroom thing never mattered anyway, because inevitably there was always at least one student who didn't listen and would complain loudly on the bus about how much they had to go. Then the bus would need to finally stop just for them, and all of the kids would jump out turning it into a half hour pit stop. But, this was also something prepared and calculated for on the road. I had pretty much every angle covered when it came to those little intangible things.

I quickly made my way over to Tyler amidst all the craziness. I fully expected him to give another excuse and say it wasn't going to work, but he didn't. He just said, "Hey, sorry I'm late." I smiled and said, "Glad you're here." I told him to hop on one of the buses and we'd head out of town. And just for good measure, I took a trip past the garbage can in the youth room where I'd sent students discreetly to unload their potential mistakes for the weekend, and sure enough there were some brownies, pills, flasks of alcohol and even a couple bags of weed. That never failed. It's amazing how honest students become when they feel respected and not judged. And it's also amazing how honest they become when they feel worried and busted.

We were finally on the bus and ready for the, traffic-willing, three and a half hour bus ride up into the mountains. I took a seat near the front of the bus with a quiet kid named Steve, but I definitely noticed Tyler sitting in the back of the bus with his hood up and ipod on. It was just good to see him there, and I didn't make a fuss over the fact that we specifically said no ipods. I know it's hard to have double-standards, but truth be told sometimes it happens, and in this unique case it was all right with me.

The bus ride was fun. Those always tend to go pretty quickly considering the amount of options you have for talking to a variety of different people and the endless car games that you can play and make up. We made one up called "The Celebrity Game" which was pretty fun, and not one bit complicated. You would start with someone naming a celebrity, then go around in a circle with the next person having to name a different celebrity whose first name started with the first letter of the previous person's last name. It makes sense, but has absolutely no point other than it's fun and takes up time. Another crowd favorite that we made up was "Eye-kward," which is too meaningful to share with others, plus would not get the same rise and respect it deserves from other groups, I'm sure. And also just a movie game where you'd go back and forth, having to name a movie that started with each letter of the alphabet. Yes, we were definitely stretching our creative minds!

With all of the bus games filling up time, we arrived at camp. The kids were allowed to get off the bus in the parking lot to stretch their legs, which turned into immediate snowball fighting and sliding on the ice. In the meanwhile I took Megan, our key female counselor up to the registration shack to turn in our medical release forms and to get the keys to our cabins. After finding out where we were going to be staying, we made the students get their luggage and head off to their cabins. The girls grumbled a little about having to walk so far to their cabins, but the guys didn't seem to notice the distance since they were all so excited. Chad and I along with our other guy leader, Derek unlocked our three adjoining cabins and let the guys choose wherever they wanted to sleep. The guys were a little bit easier going about that stuff from what I heard from the girls' side, but they also had to abide by our leader rule, which was that Chad, Derek and I got to trump any student and pick any bed we wanted, so they should choose wisely. We had nineteen guys, so about six to a room. I chose the room that Tyler was going to be in. That was the room with the older guys, including Landon and some others that I was connecting with. Tyler had remained quiet, but at least Landon was there to reach out a friendly conversation which I'm sure helped Tyler out, since he was still visibly anxious.

Over the next hour and a half the students had some free time. Some of them already knew the drill since they'd come every year, so they'd head to the game room or do the traditional push-up contest or whatever. I took that time to try and be intentional about speaking with every guy in our group, just to tell them I was happy they were there. It was a lot easier up at camp than it'd been at the church, and most of my anxiety went away once the buses left the parking lot.

The meal time was good. It was great to see all of the students there and get a real feel for what to expect over the next couple of days. We had a chance to meet the camp director and the speaker for the weekend before dinner at a counselor's meeting. They seemed great and the message series sounded cool, the theme was "Identity," meaning in Christ and what that looks like. And the food was good as well, typical camp food, but actually better than I'd had at other camps. After dinner we didn't even need to scrape, stack and sort because there was a student-led kitchen crew that was there that weekend, just to serve all of us! That was cool.

After dinner we all made it, eventually, into the auditorium room. I say eventually because there was a group of freshman guys that apparently got lost and "didn't know" where we all went, and somehow ended up back in their cabin. It was curious how they didn't notice the entire flock of 600-plus campers and leaders heading in a herd to the same exact building directly after we finished eating. But I was happy to be the one to find them and help re-direct them to where we were at. I'm not a huge disciplinarian, but I do use a lot of sarcasm; it is one of my gifts. I also use opportunities for discipline as chances to teach, not to punish. Something I learned from my dad. I'm also not a huge fan of conflict, which I don't feel many are, but I tried to stay pretty clear from that unless I really needed to drop the hammer, which I could do.

Once in the auditorium, we all sat as a large group right up front and center. We had a lot of loud student leaders who really embraced the camp thing and got everyone encouraged and pumped up. I was thankful for that. We took up the first few steps of the room. During each transition though, I found myself keeping an eye on Tyler. Not because I thought I'd catch him doing something bad, but because I was hoping he'd get something out of the weekend. And it wasn't because I told him I'd pay for his trip if he didn't, I had some guilt inside that he was going to be miserable and felt that maybe I had pushed him too hard to be there. I even found myself struggling with thoughts of maybe this wasn't the right time or place for Tyler. I had to keep reminding myself that it wasn't about me and praying that God had a plan in store.

The session started and it was loud in there! They were a crazy bunch of high school students with a ton of energy after being cramped on a bus all afternoon and now having full stomachs and around a lot of new faces. It was awesome! The camp folks did a great job right from the start. They didn't start by just standing up and giving rules. No one would've listened. So, they started exactly how you would expect; they blared the new Taylor Swift song over the loud speakers. Everyone went nuts, including most of the guys, and jumped around as they played that "Tonto, Jump on it," song, the one that goes, "Da. Da. Dah. Dah. Dah. Dah. Tonto, jump on it, jump on it." It was a crowd pleaser and always catchy.

Then things got pretty weird when a dude came out on stage dressed as Chewbaca and a girl dressed as Miley Cyrus. That got everyone's attention as Miley proceeded to hold a conversation and would translate Chewy's R-rolling speech. I have to admit, it was good comedy and the kids all liked it. Then they showed a pretty impressive and equally as funny rules video. Which got to the point, but did it in a memorable way. Because let's face it, no one wanted to listen to some person reading a list of rules, but when it was put in the context of a story, it was something they wouldn't forget. They did a good job of transitioning out of that and then brought out the band. The band was really talented and sounded great. They played a few high energy songs and then played a couple others that brought the level down a notch. Music always has a great way of changing the atmosphere. By the end of their set, the place was quiet and everyone was sitting, ready to hear what the camp speaker had to say. He was introduced and took the stage.

He had a commanding presence and it was evident right away that he had a great sense of humor. It was something that really drew everybody in. Throughout his talk he used personal life stories and humor, but had the ability to stop on a dime with a serious note. The message was about where our worth as people comes from. He showed many examples about how since the Fall of Adam and Eve, we'd become a group of people that is constantly comparing and competing with each other. And the idea that our lives are filled with ups and downs based on how others' words and actions make us feel at the time, both positive and negative. It's a crazy rollercoaster life if that's all we're basing things on, and all of the feelings of praise and negativity always wear off at some point, and that we should be seeking something more, something that's lasting. Ultimately that's God and our identity is found in Him who's our creator. Again, he used humorous, relevant stories for high school kids and adults, but also backed up everything he was talking about with Scripture. He had a huge list of verses that tell us who we really are, and who God tells us that we are in the Bible and why that's so important. At least that's what I got from the talk.

That's what was cool about camp and interpreting messages in any capacity, is that everyone hears it differently. So after the talk we were set free to go back to our cabins and have discussion time.

They handed the leaders a list of questions as we all shuffled out the doors into the now very noticeable cold, mountain air.

When we got back to the cabin area with all the guys, they took a few minutes to go to the bathroom and find their Bibles, and to my surprise, at least eight or ten of them had actually remembered to bring them, which was impressive. Since it was the first night and it all felt new in many ways to all of us, even if we'd done it before, it wasn't with each other. So I had us all meet in one large group. The kids got settled into a very cramped room, with twenty-two guys crowding onto three separate bunk beds and finding every open spot on the floor.

I started off by asking what everyone thought about the day in general. There were a few surface comments like, "The bus was tight." "It was funny when Tim slipped on the ice," and "When Brady farted on Sarah." Good stuff, and for a lot of the kids, that's really what camp was about and that was all right. I could relate. Some of my best memories of youth trips in high school had everything to do with inside jokes and things that happened outside of the actual program. This is a huge reason why camps and retreats worked so well, kids were allowed to be kids.

I continued to try and dig a little deeper than embarrassing falls and the wonderful tactic of courting girls with flatulence. So, I said, "As far as camp stuff so far, what have you liked, and did you get anything from the speaker tonight?" The answers for that were good too, I heard a bunch of the kids say, "Yeah, the speaker is bomb" and "The worship is way good." The thing about debriefing, especially with a group that size is that you allow the students to speak freely about what they are really feeling, but more importantly, process in their heads what's going on, even if they don't say a word. I was conscious of that as I continued on with our discussion. I wanted to let the guys have an opportunity to express what they were feeling, even if at that time it was internal. I had glanced over the sheet of questions that the camp staff had given us to use, then promptly shoved it back into my pocket. No disrespect for their questions, but I wanted our conversation to take a natural progression.

We talked for a good thirty or forty minutes, which was pretty cool, considering it was the first night and there was still an over-abundance of energy that all of the guys were ready to use, and they knew as soon as we were done it was free time until bed. And it never helps when you start hearing people talking and walking by your cabin. Not only was it distracting, but it gives you this sense that there's something going on outside that you can't see and you are missing out! I used to feel that way in high school when we were waiting for the bell to ring and I always seemed to have that one teacher that made you sit and actually wait for it at that last hour of the day, while everyone else got let out early and was walking by your class. I guess taking on the role of teacher had made me sensitive to those situations too.

As our conversation was winding down however, I gave the final call for any questions or comments. I did it only as a formality with the sense that nobody would speak, but then I heard a faint question from the other side of the room. "So, why does it matter what God thinks about me?" Everyone stopped what they were doing, and there was this sense that everyone settled back down. Tyler, who had been sitting quietly in the corner on the top of a bunk bed the entire time, and seemed to be tuned out, spoke up and asked a very blunt and honest question. I wanted to clarify it and hear his thoughts, so I repeated it and said, "Why do *you* think it matters?" He answered with a pretty sharp tone saying, "I don't really think it does. I mean if it did, then I'm screwed. Since I'm sure God hates me."

Ugh. Ouch. Those words just pierce my heart. To hear someone say they view God as hateful has gotten a poor message and a skewed sampling.

I didn't respond with the typical churchy response of "No, God Loves You." Although that was true, he gave a real response and I wanted to give a real answer in that moment, so I continued with a question. "Why do you think God hates you?" Now this conversation had gotten serious pretty fast, and I'm sure that half of the guys were getting uncomfortable and the other half just antsy to leave, but it was important and I never wanted to miss out on a teachable moment.

Tyler's response was again negative and a little condescending, but also very authentic, "Well, I party and swear and all that, I'm not a virgin and I don't like many people cause they piss me off. I've got a very short temper, and like to fight."

It came off as tough, but sincere. It was obvious that the comment had a lot to do with building up his insecurities, but also bearing a burden in his soul, hence the reason we were still sitting there.

I looked around at the guys, who now had seemed a little more interested and settled than a few minutes ago. I was ready to teach for a minute. I had been given the green light and asked them if they'd give five to ten more minutes. This was good stuff, and it was rare to have such a candid audience in a unique setting like that. They all agreed and did so with a sense of intrigue.

This was a chance for me to get on a soap box a little; it was a question and comment that deserved a meaningful response. It felt like a good opportunity to set the record straight on such a common misconception that I think people and students have a lot about the "God doesn't like me, because I'm bad," theory. There is a big difference between God not liking our actions and God not liking us. I always wondered how you could read a love story like the Bible and miss the blatant point of God's love and desire for us. So I went for it. These kids hadn't seen me speak in such a fired up way before, but I was ready to give a little taste of what that looked like. I had a hard time keeping emotions inside of me when it came to such an important topic:

> *All right dudes, buckle up. I want to talk for a few minutes regarding the comment made about God not liking you. Where does that come from? Did God ever say that? Or does that thought come from somewhere else?*

Because I've seen that a lot. I've seen people and students who have this perception of God that in order for God to love them or to be a Christian, it's just about following rules. Those rules being, don't drink, don't swear, don't sleep around and all of those other things that our society has labeled as "fun." But I have to say that I haven't heard God ever talk about us having to be a certain way to be loved by Him. In the Scriptures I haven't heard Him say that once you are this way or that, THEN I will love you. God loves us no matter what. Period. You guys need to hear that, and really understand it. God loves YOU no matter what.

Now because of how much we're loved, here's what God did for us, He gave His son Jesus to die in place of our sins which was the most amazing thing He could ever do. Think about that, He had His own son beaten to death and put on a cross, so we could live a full life and be free from the punishment of sin! He was sacrificed for our sins. I know a lot of you know that and get that, but do you really understand it? Because here's the deal: Once we understand what God did for us, once we realize how much He loves us and who He's called us to be, and that He's in control, we hopefully won't have any other response but to love Him and follow Him with our whole lives! The Bible says, "There is therefore now no condemnation for those who are in Christ Jesus" (Rom. 8:1). That means all the junk we deal with, and all the poor choices we make in life are all made good through

Jesus! It's like getting convicted of a crime and having someone serve the sentence for you. Even though we're good people, we're all guilty of sin against God, that's just how it is in our world unfortunately. And that's not being negative to put us down or give us fear, that's just being realistic and should actually give us hope and excitement to be given that love and grace!

Once we realize what He did for us and what the reward in heaven is, we shouldn't have any other way of responding than living a life that honors God, and when we honor others and live a life like Jesus, then we honor God. Being a Christian is about living a life in response to the gift that God has given us. When we make the choice to give our lives back over to the one who gave it to us in the first place, things make more sense. It's not just a one time decision that comes from some sort of formula, but it's a decision to be Like Christ in everything that we do and every decision we make. He loves us so much that He wants our lives to matter. And at some point you guys will all need to ask the question of yourself, "How do I want my life to matter and what does that look like?"

Our lives matter and they should look like Jesus. Don't just listen to what I say either, but read the Bible for yourselves, ask tough questions and seek out answers! That's what I have done in my own life and came to this conclusion.

It's backwards when people say "God doesn't love me, cause I'm bad, or I can't be a Christian because I do all of these bad things." What it really should be about is recognizing what He's done for you and respond by not offending Him or doing the things He's said will get in the way of our relationship with Him. Because this whole thing is about a relationship, not a bunch of religious stuff. See, the things we sometimes look at as rules, are really things that can make us stumble and keep our eyes off of God. God wants us to have a fulfilling life! Once we fall in love with God, we won't want to do the things that will harm us or offend Him! God says "If you love me, you will obey what I command" (John 14:15). NOT, obey all of my commands and you'll get to heaven. That's what a lot of people want to know, how much do I need to do, just to get to heaven, and it has nothing to do with loving God.

Look at two things you guys. Check this out. So if God tells us; don't get drunk, don't sleep around, don't steal, don't kill each other etc. what He's really saying is that our lives will be much better if we aren't walking down a road that holds us down and can lead to destructive things. How many of you can say that stealing has ever been great?! There was never any guilt or hurt feelings, or that sleeping around never ended up with hurt emotions and brokenness. Killing people? Is that a good thing? Those are the things that God is telling us to stay away from, because they are destructive and not the way we're meant to live. And He would know, He created us!

The other thing is this: So, what would it look like to my wife, if she was telling me all the time to go get her a nice blinged out ring. And then one morning she said bluntly, "Please, if you love me, buy me a nice ring today after you get done with work." So I do, and hand her the ring after work, tell her "Here's what you requested" and walk away. Is that real love? Or am I just responding to what her request was to make her happy? I didn't come up with that idea out of the love and thoughtfulness in my heart...

Is the ring something that she even wants now?

But, what if I'm so head over heels in love with my wife and I know she would love a ring, but she never has to tell me to buy one for her, and one day I walk through a park because I'm thinking about her and then head over to a jewelry store, look for an hour, buy her the perfect ring and then leave it on the table for her in the morning when she wakes up with a sweet little poem that I wrote for her. It means something different right? Because what she cares about is my heart and not just doing stuff out of guilt or obligation. It's not about the ring. The ring is just a symbol, but my action speaks my real heart and love.

I love my wife, therefore, I don't want to offend or hurt her by doing the things that would harm our relationship. Like when she tells me not to date other people. Yeah, that would harm our relationship, and I don't want to do that, so if I see a pretty girl and am tempted, I stay away because my wife is so much better!

(Now by this point my voice is cracking with emotion, I'm barely spitting words out and my eyes are filled with passionate tears.)

*Guys, it's the same with God. He has called and showed us the right way to live through His example in Jesus, but He wants us to **want** to live that way because we are so in love with Him. Which means we don't go to church just to sit there because it's the right thing to do and do it out of obligation, or we think that'll get us to heaven, no, we seek out God's love for us, fall madly in love with our creator, understand the reward and life He's offered and look so forward to the opportunity to go to church and worship Him out of a real desire in our heart.*

Guys, be assured that in Romans 5:8 it says, "But God demonstrates his own love for us in this: While we were still sinners, Christ died for us." This says how much we're loved and tells us that "while we were and ARE still sinners, Christ died for us." If we were all perfect, there wouldn't have been any need. Our life comes through His death and resurrection!

Do you love God? Do you know God? Do

you know that your life matters? My prayer is that all of you fall in love with or have fallen in love with God. And it breaks my heart to hear that you'd view yourself as not good enough and therefore God wants nothing to do with you. I've got a word for you, if God based things on our "perfect" living then none of us would be good enough. That's what grace means. The Bible is filled with stories of people that lied, slept around, murdered people etc. that God used in powerful ways after they fell in love with Him and had a life transformation. We aren't any different than them. But we can live in a way where we seek to live a perfect life like Christ did. We are broken and through Jesus are saved to do His will in our lives!

So, the question was, "Why does it matter what God thinks about me"? The answer simply put, is that you matter so much that God became a man to show us how to live and was willing to die for you to give you life not to take it away...

It was a moment where I had no idea of where what I had just said came from. I had gone on for a good ten minutes with something burning in my heart preaching the gospel and I wasn't sure what the response would be. All I knew was that it was God speaking through me.

The room was quiet. Maybe some were in shock over how all of that just poured out of me, maybe some had totally fallen asleep. But the first words I heard after that were, "Dude. Tight." I don't even know who said it, but it broke the tension some and the guys all laughed. Then they started moving around and joking.

I thanked them for letting me speak and that what I just said was the essence of the entire Christian faith. It's about being who we are and loving a relentless God who's created us to be His. And there wasn't anything we could do that would make Him love us less. Being a follower of Christ is all about recognizing what God has done for us, His love for us and His desire for us to live a life honoring and loving Him and others. It's all about living a life with an appropriate response to an amazing, unconditional and eternal gift.

I gave the guys the option to head to free time or to stay and keep talking. Most of them headed out for the game room and a night game of snow football, but Tyler and a few of the older guys stayed back. We spent awhile talking a lot deeper that night. Looking back, it was one of the most important nights in my life as a youth pastor, only to be followed the next day by one of the most important nights in Tyler's life. Dang, I was so happy I had chosen to not use the official camp questions that night.

It took awhile for everyone to fall asleep. The random powerfulness of our conversations lingered for a bit, but ultimately gave way to deeper guy talk issues, such as girls, movies and sports. Everybody in my cabin finally started falling asleep around 2:00 a.m. that night. Me, however, I probably got an hour or so of rest. I'm a light sleeper anyway, and I always kept one eye open with a group of high school guys. Plus, I had a lot of things on my mind coupled with the adrenaline from before. I was emotionally drained and tired, but just couldn't sleep.

9

The Door Opens

"Believing in God is as much like falling in love as
it is making a decision. Love is both something that
happens to you and something you decide upon."
– Donald Miller, *Blue Like Jazz: Nonreligious
Thoughts on Christian Spirituality*

The next day started off well. We all ate a good breakfast and went into a small group teaching time led by the staff. By late morning we were ready to start the camp games! They had prepared large group games out on the field. The field itself had a little snow on it, but during the day it got up to about fifty degrees, so the little left was virtually gone from the field which had been pretty beaten up by a steady diet of high schoolers trampling on it for the past few months.

We had a larger group than the rest, so we only had to be paired with one other church to make a team. They were cool and their church was about fifteen minutes away from ours back home, so it was fun for our students to get to know each other a little. The games started out with some relays, obstacle courses and things of that nature. It was all just a lot of loud and controlled chaos. It was plain fun; didn't matter what we were doing, only that we were doing it together. They were also giving us props and points for putting team cheers together. I got right into it and flashed my skills, if you could call it that, by teaching a few dances to the kids. Two of my specialties were, "Sea-legs and Scrambled Eggs" and "Walk through the window, put on a sweater." I looked ridiculous.

Another game we played was a battle of strengths game with guys vs. guys and girls vs. girls. Each group was to send out their top three strongest or most athletic guys and girls. The students on each team got to pick them, and did so quickly. They easily knew who was who; it was pretty fascinating to watch. The consensus top six got ready and ran onto the field.

One of the guys from our team was Tyler, which wasn't surprising. Although he had been pretty quiet in all of the social settings so far, it was clear that all the students liked and respected him. I knew he had some leadership capabilities from having been around him on the soccer field, and it almost looked like he was enjoying the game atmosphere. He was a competitor after all. Plus, like all the others, he embraced the attention and looked a little bit more serious than he probably should've. That was the likeness of a hormonal teen, and the energy was undeniable.

The game was kind of a triathlon. It had dodge ball, tug-of-war and running, all worked into a five minute session. It was creative. The girls were up first and our team shouted our lungs out as the fierce competitors got in line to start their sprints. When the horn blew, off the girls ran, one from each team. There were four teams and three girls each to split up the duties. We took second place in the sprint part, and also second in both the tug-of-war and one-on-one dodge ball game. There was good team chemistry flowing and I'm sure somewhere down the mountain you could hear the loud chants for miles.

Next up were the guys. Our three guys had gotten each other pumped up by shoving and yelling at each other. It was close to what an NFL locker room probably looks like right before game time. Everyone was now cheering even louder. I think in part because the guys had way too much testosterone, but also because everyone had watched the girls, so they knew how it was going to flow.

The whistle blew and this guy Ryan, who was from the other church on our team, took off like a gazelle. He probably won that race around the field by a good five seconds. Our team went crazy! There was a wild Lambeau leap type thing Ryan did when he continued his winning sprint right back into our team. This built up into the next game which was the tug-of-war. There was a guy named Scotty who was in our group, he had come up with our church, but I didn't know him very well. He was a real nice kid, very quiet and polite. He also happened to be six foot four, and weighed 310 pounds. From what I'd heard, he was being pursued by division one college football programs, but really didn't like football and wasn't interested. So basically, he was a nice kid, who was just kind of a genetic freak.

He did seem to have an aggressive side though, which I thought would give us an edge in the tug-of-war. It's too bad that he eventually had to compete against a guy who happened to be six foot six, 325 pounds, and who actually did play football and was going to play at USC the next fall. So, after a valiant effort, Scotty and our team took second place. We were still in the running for the prestigious prize of getting to eat dinner first if Tyler could score the team one more first place finish in dodge ball.

Tyler trotted out to the field looking comfortable, as if he'd done this before. But he also looked a little too intense. I kept thinking jeesh, this is church camp, not the Olympics. It was partly his natural demeanor along with the buildup he got from all of the attention and encouragement from our team and atmosphere. It was a one-on-one tournament of dodge ball, and Tyler was up first. He took out the first guy that he faced almost right away. On only his second throw he hit the guy in the gut with the ball, the guy bobbled it and the ball fell just past his fingertips as he did his best diving attempt to save it. Tyler immediately turned to the team with both fists raised in the air and neck bulging out as his face turned red while screaming at the top of his lungs! He walked through about seven guys giving aggressive chest bumps the entire way.

After a few more rounds and two more wins for Tyler, it was time for the final match. The guy on the speaker, who was announcing the event, called for the two guys still competing to get back out there. The other kid, Tyler's opponent, was already standing there, ready. But Tyler was still lost in his energy and excitement giving knuckle pounds to his teammates.

For me it was cool to see him get into it, but to others who didn't know him, it was probably a little uncomfortable. It didn't help when the announcer said over the speakers, "OK, where is the guy that just won? Come back out here 'steroid boy'."

That offended Tyler as he scowled and swore towards the announcer. It was a good thing the crowd was still being so loud, because nobody really heard it, but he told the story with his body language.

As he got out there and seemed to get settled in, the ref played to the crowd a little bit by pumping it up that the winner of this would determine the overall winner for the morning and they'd get to have their team eat dinner first, which was pretty synonymous with winning the Stanley Cup or Super Bowl I suppose. It was all in good fun, and the guys got into position.

At this point, Tyler still looked pretty intense so I ran out close to him and got his attention. When he looked at me, I said "Remember; Dodge, Duck, Dip, Dive and Dodge. And hey, if you can dodge a wrench, you can dodge a ball." These were two great quotes from the movie *Dodgeball* and it got a roar from the crowd. I wanted to lighten the mood for Tyler who turned away from me without any sort of response, just a determined face looking like he had something to prove.

The two guys got into position and both held a ball about twenty feet apart from each other. The ref blew the whistle and within two seconds Tyler had taken five steps forward and went to fire the ball. But when he stepped to throw, he slipped on a small patch of ice, consequently dropping the ball in mid-throw and falling to the ground. All within another couple of seconds, the other guy fired a ball that hit Tyler in the face as he struggled to gain his footing and he fall back again. Everyone laughed at the situation, and the kid that threw the ball was heading off to celebrate. But Tyler, having been knocked to the ground and thinking he'd been made fun of by the announcer moments ago, stood up with a mission. He must have assumed the guy that threw the ball at his face did so intentionally and then laughed at him. It was blown out of proportion in Tyler's mind, but he was embarrassed and hurt. Everyone was laughing at the situation, but he thought they were laughing at him. So, he did what he thought would help him save some face and ran up behind the guy and shoved him from the back, knocking him to the ground yelling "C'mon let's go, bitch!"

He used a few more choice words and challenged him to either a rematch or fight, maybe both, it wasn't very clear. The kid, who was caught off guard said, "Hey man, I'm sorry, I'm sorry."

This "all in fun" game had evolved into something different for Tyler. I had a sense that the emotion was about a lot of things, and not just that specific moment. Before anything else could happen, I intervened along with a few other leaders and counselors. I told Tyler, in a calm voice, "Hey, let's go take a walk."

The rest of the students were left stunned. Nobody really understood what had happened or why it escalated to the point that it did. The camp staff did their best to diffuse the situation and started telling everyone to head to lunch in their very encouraging and friendly campy tones. I took Tyler on a little walk away from everyone to let him cool down. This was a kid who was searching for something. He needed an outlet, and he had a longing for something more than where his life was at.

The rest of that day was pretty relaxed. After lunch was free time for the remainder of the afternoon and then we met back up for dinner. I personally took the afternoon to read a little bit, take a nap and hang out with a few kids and leaders. It finally felt like the typical laid back camp feel. Plus, there was so much space up there, that when hundreds of people were scattered all around, it almost seemed isolated. Everyone got back together as we sat down for dinner and afterward headed on to the evening gathering.

The gathering was the same as the previous night for the most part. It was very high energy, with some deeper worship, and the same program staff doing entertaining skits. You could sense that after only twenty-four hours, people were settled in and it felt as though we'd been there for days. The speaker came out and did honestly one of the best talks I've ever heard in my life. And I'd heard a lot of talks, especially when they were directed at students. I had personally prepared and delivered talks weekly, for the previous seven or eight years. Therefore, I knew what a gift it was when a speaker and teacher stood out the way this guy did.

It's very rare that you can have an entire group of high schoolers hanging on your every word, where you can literally hear a pin drop from the other side of the room during a pause.

His talk that night spoke to so many students, but it also spoke to me as a leader. I wasn't immune to the convicting message of his words.

He talked about the story in Luke where Jesus heals the paralyzed man. Now, that's a pretty well known story, so I'm sure a lot in the room had heard it before, but not in the way he spoke about it. That's the story where this man had been waiting thirty-eight years to be healed from paralysis, and then he had an encounter with Jesus. He asked Jesus to help him into the pool (where he would be healed) because he couldn't jump into it on his own when the water swirled. The first person in when the water swirled would supposedly be cleansed and healed. Jesus responded with this question, "Do you want to be saved?" Isn't that question so obvious? He'd been paralyzed for thirty-eight years! But Jesus asked the question because it might not have been that obvious. The convicting part or teaching piece of the talk had to do with our lives and our struggles, and how often times we might just be so used to the way things are, that we really don't want to be saved or rescued from our junk. It was enlightening. It was real. It was a full hour of a talk that you wish you could've heard another hour of.

It was one of those talks that almost made you jealous deep down because you wish you could've been the one delivering it. God was working in that man and it was being received openly and lives were being changed forever in that place right in front of our eyes.

During that entire talk I had my eyes focused on the speaker, but my heart was searching around the room for these students. I kept picturing each student's face and praying they were really hearing this message and getting something out of it and wondering if their eyes were welling up with tears, like mine were. I had a hard time knowing what the tears even meant. I wasn't sure if they were tears of conviction, tears of passion, tears of grace, or maybe a combination of all of those, but the one thing I knew was that they were real. How many times had I heard talks that I was just numb to? There had been too many to count that lacked substance, and were too light and fluffy. Therefore, I recognized the magnitude of what was happening that night.

As soon as the talk was over and the speaker prayed, we were told to get into our church groups to discuss and debrief what we'd heard. I immediately scoped out our kids so I could see their reactions and confirm if it was anything like my own. And to no surprise, there wasn't a single kid who wasn't in some sort of a zone, processing what had been heard. And then I noticed that I didn't see Tyler. I knew originally he was in the room that night, but he wasn't anymore. He was one I had been picturing throughout the talk, wondering how the message was hitting his ears and heart, and now it seemed as though he'd missed the entire thing.

On complete instinct I told Chad and Megan to just start chatting with the students and breaking things down with them as I headed out to look for Tyler. It was all biblical that night as I went looking for the one lost sheep.

After a few minutes I found Tyler a little ways away from the amphitheater where we'd been earlier in the day. He was alone, sitting on a concrete post staring out at the cold lake water in the moonlight and smoking a cigarette. At that moment, I could've cared less that he was smoking. My feet led me right to the rickety post adjacent to him. I sat down calmly and silently. He saw me, but didn't budge or panic. After the morning games session he disengaged himself from everything going on around him, and he still seemed distant now. I'm not sure if it was sulking or annoyance, but either way there was some sort of conflict in his soul happening.

I sat down by him and here is how our conversation went:

Evan: Hey man, so how long have you been out here?

Tyler: A few minutes.

E: Did you happen to catch the worship stuff?

T: Yeah, I was in there, so you don't have to worry.

E: I wasn't worried; so what's going on, how has your day been?

(He gave me a look that either said, "are you kidding me?" or that he was about to break down.)

T: Life is just so F-ed up you know?

E: Yeah, trust me, I know.

T: You don't know. You've got this perfect life, probably never done anything wrong, how the hell do you think you can understand me? I'm sure you'll call my mom to come and pick me up too, cause of this thing...

As he held the cigarette in front of my face, I had no other choice in the world. I wanted to connect with Tyler that night. A compelling sense took over and on the spot, as he was finishing his sentence that was defining a boundary between our lives; I broke the wall down as I snatched the cigarette from his hand. He was startled because it was so abrupt and I'm sure had a fleeting thought I was going to smash it on the ground and run to the phone. But before he could dwell on that thought, I put it up to my mouth and took a puff, which probably looked as awkward as it felt because I wasn't a smoker. But as Tyler sat back in awe, I handed the cigarette back to him, almost as if passing the peace pipe, and I said...

E: It's not about this. It's not about a cigarette; it's about your heart, your life. It's so much bigger than that. God has so many things He's going to do in your life, He's just waiting for you to get onboard with it all. He doesn't need you. He wants you.

At that point, everything stood still. Something happened and Tyler broke down, verbally and physically. It wasn't scary, it was incredible. He started crying and speaking with his volume getting louder and more strained with each thing he started pouring out.

T: God. Where is God?! Where's He been?! He doesn't care about me! He doesn't hear me! Why does he make me question Him so much?! Why did He make my dad an alcoholic?! Why am I always so frustrated?!

The list kept going on, and I was humbled to be a part of watching God work in this way in Tyler's heart. He was doing some cleansing of his soul to prepare room for God to come in; the only thing I was doing was praying. I put my hand on his shoulder as he continued an outpouring of emotional junk that had held him hostage. And after each thing he let go of, I kept repeating to him in a soft voice, "God can handle it. God can handle it. God can handle it." And over and over as he kept going, until he finished on this:

T: Why does God allow us pain and WHY Did God take my brother Jacob?!!

It was booming. It was climactic. It was very honest and authentic. Tyler stopped then with a sense that he had really been heard, and it wasn't just by me. A sense of calmness came over him as we sat in silence for a few minutes before we started talking again.

That night we stayed out for at least another hour talking. The only reason we eventually stopped was because our group had sent out a search party for us!

Tyler shared stuff that he had never talked about before and I opened up about my personal stuff too. He told me about his identical twin brother, Jacob who had drowned a couple years before that on a church camping trip. This was something that I had never known. It was also the reason Tyler had completely turned away from the church because he blamed God. And this was why his father had started drinking so much and why he watched his parents' marriage fall apart right before his eyes, although they still "put on a pretty good show" as he stated.

He told me that night that He didn't want to blame God anymore. He had heard everything the speaker had said, and his answer was "Yes." He wanted to be saved from the reckless and unfulfilling life he'd been leading and saw in his future. He was ready for something more.

As soon as we left the spot and were walking away, I said the only thing that I had left to say to him that night, "You know they give you cancer, right?" I said with a half-hearted smile. He looked at me with the same grin and said, "Yeah, I've heard that."

The next night, which was our last, we had a powerful worship sesh. And as I looked around the room, I spotted Tyler, with his hands up in the air belting out the words "My life be lifted high," and I looked at Chad who had been watching the same thing and we just mouthed the words "No Way" to each other. This was not the same kid I had to beg to come to camp.

—⁂—

We went home the next day and came to a parking lot where there was a huge fanfare of parents and friends to welcome us back. In the crowd I saw Tyler's parents. I knew a little bit more now as he walked up and hugged both of them simultaneously with one arm around each. There were many parents and students that came and thanked me for a good trip and for leading, but the one I remember the most is when Tyler came up, gave me a bro hug and said, "Don't worry man, you don't have to pay me back."

10

Down The Mountain

"First they ignore you, then they laugh at you, then
they fight you, then you win."
– Mohandas Gandhi

There's something about having an intimate retreat away that doesn't translate when you get back to regular life. By that, I mean it's hard to have someone who didn't experience what you did, completely understand what you had gone through. That's part of the uniqueness and excitement about camps, retreats or vacations, but it can also be very frustrating. Before we left camp I had a good talk with the kids about that. I told them to not expect others to give you the response you are looking for, because they haven't had the same experience. Your friends won't understand exactly what the moments felt like, what the cabins smelled like or any of the inside jokes. This has always been a difficult thing in general, but definitely in youth ministry. They call it a mountain top experience, and this time it literally was. The other thing I wanted to encourage the kids with was to not let others' responses take away anything that they experienced up at camp. Again, that's hard to do, no matter if its a couple days away or a couple of weeks. The harsh reality of the spiritual high felt after those events eventually dwindled down and in most cases away.

I had experienced that many times in my personal life. Whether it was a powerful retreat, sports tournament or just a vacation, it was always hard to translate the feelings and personal experiences into dramatic enough words for people to fully understand and bring people back into the moment with you. We want people to experience things just as we have, in the same way we did. The key as I mentioned, was to not let the routine of life strip away at the raw emotion of an experience. That was something I was going to have to deal with personally too. And of course, all I kept thinking about was how Tyler's life would change or stay the same. I felt a calm sense that his experience was real and things would be much different for him from then on. And so was the wrap up on camp.

—m—

I came home to my beautiful wife whom I felt that I hadn't seen in a couple of weeks. I waited at least two hours that night before I mentioned a word about the trip. And even when I finally did, I only dropped bits and pieces here and there, to the responses of "Really?" "That's cool," and "OK." All were polite, and that's all I expected. She cared a lot about my experience at camp and I knew at some point would want all the details, but in that moment, she was just happy to have me back, and I was glad to be home.

Those were the first nights that I had stayed away from JoHanna since we'd moved to California, but the cool thing about spending time away for work is that I was able to take the next few days off to recoup.

We took a couple of days to reconnect and live out all of our dreams on Splash Mountain at Disneyland. One of the best things about Southern California is Disneyland. I am a huge fan of that place, but I have to admit I thought going there regularly would take away a lot of the "magic." It really didn't. We had bought season passes, which was cool because we could go in the evenings for a few hours to walk around and not have to feel guilty about wasting money. We even got a little snobby with it and when lines were over a fifteen minute wait, we just said, nah, and walked away. The traffic was even growing on us a little bit. We were now far less frustrated sitting in traffic than when we'd first gotten to SoCal because we accepted that that was the way it was and adjusted our plans accordingly.

Some of our other favorite activities were becoming routine at that time too. It seemed that every opportunity we had to be together and go do stuff, we would choose something from the growing list of our favorites. We loved the ocean and really liked finding new beaches. I had even started surfing. My goal was to find every beach that was mentioned in the song "Surfin' USA" by the Beach Boys.

We definitely had our regular beaches though, complete with nearby grocery or convenience stores where we'd buy donuts and milk for the morning walk. Yes, our routine was definitely forming. It felt good. I think after working a lot harder in our relationship and getting closer, along with feeling more comfortable in my job and that I was making a connection, California was truly starting to feel like home for us. That was a good feeling because we both continued to struggle with bouts of homesickness, but it was becoming less frequent. We never took for granted the weather in California either. And we also never missed out on a good chance to rub it in with our friends and family back in Minnesota. C'mon, we deserved to a little bit.

It was safe to say that life was going well. The rest of that week, I took it easy. I was around church some, but didn't try to over do it. After working really hard on maintaining a healthy work schedule that was producing results at work, I was also seeing positive ones in my personal life.

I had been anticipating youth group that week much more than usual because of the connection I was making, and the excitement I had to hear how everyone else had been doing after their personal experience at camp.

Youth group felt like a reunion of sorts. Most of the students showed up who had gone to camp, and the majority of them hadn't been there before, so that was cool. I wasn't naïve in thinking that the number of kids there would last, it was expected the week after camp for there to be a big crowd, but it was still encouraging to see. I was however, a little disappointed in not seeing Tyler there.

We spent the night talking over memories from camp and trying to rekindle a little bit of the spiritual fire. It turned into mostly reminiscing about funny memories like when Stacy slipped on the stairs in front of the dining center and 100 other students watched, and when Trevor dropped a two-pound block of ice down the back of Grady's shirt, you know, those kinds of things. But it was all good and relationships were being strengthened.

The last thing I told the kids that night, was to never forget that experience and for those who didn't go, I hoped they'd get a chance to in the future. Then I promised them that I had it in my heart to make sure that every week when we met up it would feel as close to that camp experience as possible. Things were going to happen and we'd continue to grow. No more of the mountain top experiences and then down. We were going to just settle up on top of that mountain within the youth program weekly. The kids were stoked. They wanted it, they wanted to go deep. It hurts to watch people not give students enough credit sometimes, or to try to "dumb down" messages for them. There's a huge difference between finding ways to relate a message to youth and dumbing it down. In my heart, every student had the right to hear about Jesus Christ. If we weren't growing, learning and surrendering, then we might as well have been a group that only met for games and activities at a local community center. There was and is something else going on that is much more important than only hanging out as a church group. It's all about growing and living a loving life of reaching out.

Later that night after youth group was over, I turned my phone back on and had a text from Tyler that said, "SRY I MISSED 2NITE, DINNER THIS WK?"

I called him back on my drive home and made plans to meet up with him that very next day.

—⁕—

This was the first time I had seen Tyler since camp, and I was pretty curious to see what, if anything, had changed in his life or if there had been any lasting effects over the past week or so. But nothing could've prepared me for the talk that we were about to have. We met up at *In N Out,* it was casual and busy as usual. After we got our food we found a table outside in a quiet little nook. It was about as private as it could've been in that situation. While we were waiting for our food we shared small talk. Tyler told me about school and groaned about homework, and also spoke about his Super Bowl predictions and his San Diego Chargers team. It was, after all, the middle of the NFL season. But for one of the first years in my life, I hadn't really noticed. I'm the biggest football fan, but it was hard to watch games when you worked on Sundays, and on top of that, the fall and winter had been an especially busy time in my life.

Throughout those minutes of small talk, I found myself trying to read deeper into the conversation. I tried to read mannerisms and see if there were any little indications that there was a change in Tyler's life. I had been praying for this kid and investing in his life now for the past few months and I was so sure that God was doing something incredible in Him. As soon as we sat down, it happened. I saw some fruits of what God had been doing. Almost immediately after his butt hit the chair he started speaking. It felt as though the past week and a half didn't exist and we were right back in continuation of our conversation at camp, which was the last time we'd really spoken. Tyler spoke with the most hopeful tone I'd heard from him yet.

T: So, I just wanted to say, sorry I didn't make it to youth group this past week, I was in a deep conversation with some friends.

(This from the kid that previously wouldn't set foot on the church grounds, let alone go to youth group, and he was apologizing. I had to smile big at that.)

E: Hey no worries. What were you chatting about?

T: Man, everything! I told them all about my time up at camp, but I was totally talking to them about life and heaven and what it all meant and where we all were going and what we were all doing, and they were all asking me questions, and I didn't know the answers, but something just told me that I did, you know? Then I opened up to them about my family, my brother, my dad, everything. And they told me stuff that I had never ever known about them. And I kept thinking that these were the closest friends I had in the world, I saw them every day and we'd gone through

everything together, yet I didn't even know the most basic and important things about their lives!

(He was literally talking a mile a minute, I was trying to keep up, but it felt more like I was trying to get a sip of water from a fire hydrant.)

He went on to talk about college and what he was going to do with his life and on most levels everything that he said had nothing specific to do with his faith, but it was all grounded in a deeply rooted spirituality. He was confused, as if all of a sudden an invisible rug had been pulled out from beneath his feet and shaken his very existence. It was so overwhelmingly an encounter with Jesus, but I just wanted to hear him say it and come to that conclusion on his own. And he did.

Tyler talked for about half an hour. I listened intently to every word that he spoke, but none of the words rang more vividly than these.

His voice slowed, and he spoke almost with a sense of exhaustion, as if he had come to the conclusion of not just his speech that he had let out, but to a conclusion of what life meant.

T: I have had a pretty decent family growing up. I have been yelled at and praised my whole life, about as much as anyone probably. I've gotten a lot of compliments too though and been told "I love you" a few times. But when we were at camp, it was the first time that I had ever really FELT loved, like really loved. So yeah, I've done some drugs, sure, and drank alcohol whatever and that's altered my moods and stuff, but this feeling that just came over me was something that I can't explain, but want more of, you know? It has ruined my week in the best way; I haven't been able to think about anything else. I haven't even thought of having a smoke or wanting to party because I've just been so messed up with the idea that I'm sick and I've wrestled

with the question "Do I want to get better?" Evan, is that God?

My heart absolutely fell out of my stomach; I was in the presence of a true life transformation. How do you respond to that? He just told me that it *was God* in everything that he said. I don't think he really needed an answer. I told him with a huge smile, "Dude, be careful, He'll ruin your life. But it's the best decision you'll ever make."

We spent the next hour talking. I shared with Tyler more of my own struggles and triumphs and how there was always this emptiness inside in either situation. I got to a point where I knew God, but didn't really pursue Him at all. So much of my faith was all in my head, but hadn't impacted my heart and wasn't on the outside yet. I was sick of merely living a life constantly competing and comparing myself with others. I told Him about God's promises to us, how Jesus lived, and when we choose to follow that, everything will change. Life with Jesus isn't just a happy people club, it's a real club! But it also offers us meaning and a purpose too. And as we'd talked about before, life with Christ isn't a life filled with no fun and only a bunch of rules, it's a life that is being lived exactly the way it was intended to be lived. And that can include struggles, sacrifices and hurt which are however, all rooted in a deep eternal sense of peace and joy! I asked Tyler questions like, "Why does it feel so good to love? Why does it feel so good to give love?" And I continued to say, "Because that's how we are wired, that's how we've been created! When we figure out that life isn't about us at all, it becomes an opportunity to be truly set free and apart from the struggles of the earth that hold us down and tell us who we are. And for me, if I want to figure out what my purpose is, wouldn't it make sense that I would ask the one that made me, instead of the kids in my gym class or on my soccer team? I've figured out that the meaning of my life is to point to God and respond to His love for me."

We were winding down on our conversation. Tyler was still very engaged and deep in thought. He wanted to be sold out on this idea, but like a lot of people was still pretty skeptical. The last two things I left Tyler with were, that following Jesus had everything to do with a relationship and it wasn't about a religion, and in our culture, God gets confused with religion too often, and a lot of the time people turn their backs on both. That statement seemed to have struck a chord in Tyler, as if he'd never once thought about it that way. Yes, that night a life was truly changed and I was blessed to have been around to watch God work.

As we were leaving, Tyler ran in to grab a to-go box, since he hadn't touched his food at all. And as we walked out to our cars, he answered his phone and the first thing out of his mouth was, "Dude, Luke, you're coming with me to church next week." I could only wonder what the response was on the other side. As Tyler tried to multi-task and explain, he reached out, looked at me with very expressive eyes and gave me the infamous bro-hug that had become our thing, and mouthed the words "Thank you," to me. Then I mouthed the words "Any Time" back to him and got into my car. As I turned on the gas, Tyler just about made me lose my bladder as he pounded on my window, urgently wanting me to roll it down. I did, and as he held his phone by his side, he asked, "Hey, will you pray for me tonight?" I responded, "Dude, I've been praying for you every night since I met you." Then I drove away.

11

A Quest With Questions

"The Church should be full of people who seek
questions rather than answers, mystery instead of
solutions, wonder instead of explanations."

"Our inability to answer all the questions became
an opportunity to learn more about God. When
our intellect fell short, our souls connected with
the reality of God. There, in our unknowing, God
showed up unexpectedly."

– Michael Yaconelli, *Dangerous Wonder*

I couldn't believe that it was Christmas time already. Our first five months had gone by very quickly in California, but there was also a lot to show for it. Five months is a long time, but it had felt much longer than that. Good things were happening all around, we felt completely adjusted as we prepared for our first Christmas without snow. I have to admit that I kind of missed the snow. The houses lit with Christmas lights around trunks of palm trees looked weird to me. And when we'd take a drive around to look at Christmas lights, we did so with the air conditioning on and sunroof open. A far cry from cranking the heater up, wearing three layers of long underwear and everyone in the car holding an ice scraper while constantly wiping off that small circle of condensation on their window for a tiny view of the outside lights. But those were some of the memories I had missed.

Having a job in a church is different in a lot of ways, and holidays seemed to be the epitome of that. Christian holidays, namely Easter and Christmas, were a time for families to have breaks and go to church. Well, working at a church means someone has to be there to provide the services. I hadn't had a Christmas Eve off for probably seven years at that point. And this year that didn't change. I was asked to read Scripture at two of the three services and also sing in a little group for the other service. Although it was Christmas time, it didn't feel like it to me, we didn't see any family that year, I had to work and JoHanna and I tried to blend our family traditions together and ended up making awful fondue that gave us both gut rot. All in all the entire Christmas experience was feeling a little bit lost to me. I felt like Charlie Brown searching for the meaning of Christmas. We did manage to keep the tradition alive by watching *National Lampoons Christmas Vacation* and *Elf*, which are two of our faves.

The week following Christmas was pretty nice, I had some time off. It wasn't technically time off, but I learned it was an unwritten rule that if we had something to do that week, we were expected to be around church, and if not, well.... Again, this came back to the ever poorly communicated job expectations, but I felt it had been a very positive fall and winter so far, therefore I didn't feel guilty having a little more time off.

During that week, the kids were off school and ironically we didn't have any youth events planned, not even our weekly youth group. However, one day when I was actually at church, I was sitting in my office looking at ESPN.com and three boys came in. It was Tyler along with Luke and Pete. I got up out of my chair excited to see them stop by out of the blue, but also just happy to see anyone since I was bored. I had always dealt with feeling guilty like I was needed somewhere when I wasn't, and that someone was looking for me when they weren't. That's why I was at least present at the church, even though nobody else was. Our minds can sort of take control over us like that sometimes.

It was really good to see those guys, and I got the impression that they were a little bit weirded out and intimidated standing in the church office, so I starting asking them what was going on as they followed me back out into the parking lot.

"Not a whole lot," Tyler said.

"We were just hanging out by the mall."

"That's cool, what's going on there?" I asked.

They all looked at each other as they said "Nothing." That's another constant I've learned about by working with students. It doesn't matter their age, city or how many friends they have, they always seemed to be bored with nothing to do. I remember feeling the same way back in the day. I guess showing up at church was something.

After the small talk they pretty much jumped right into the actual motivation for stopping by that afternoon. Tyler spoke and said, "So, we were just talking about the Bible and I was telling them what I had learned and was learning, but then we had some questions that we couldn't really answer and we thought we'd stop by." I said, "That's tight, what kind of stuff are you talking about, I'd love to hop in on the conversation." I know that I don't have all of the answers, nobody outside of God has it all figured out. Therefore, I have never wanted to come off as so arrogant to pretend I do, but at the same time, I wanted to be a part of helping shape students' own thoughts about faith and truth by sharing how I felt, what I believed and why. Not just telling them what to think and how it is. I was all about letting them figure it out on their own by helping guide them to the right places and to ask the right questions.

Luke said to me, "Well, we've never thought much about any of the stuff Tyler was telling us, it got us thinking, and the heaven stuff sounded pretty sweet. How do you get to heaven and how do you know it's right?"

That's a very common question, as it should be, especially the part about asking how do we know it's right. I'd learned this "napkin evangelism" thing years before, but I'm not sure that always works when explaining the gospel, since faith isn't about some formula. I could've said, "Well go home, do these two things, turn off the lights, count to ten in Spanish, say these words and boom! Heaven!"

But I didn't. I did however talk about our designed purpose, our separation from God, our need for a savior, our sinful nature and the hope and resurrection that Jesus promises all of us in the Bible. I told them how it's not about some religious stuff, but about talking to your creator and getting things right with Him, since it was for His pleasure that we were even made. Reciting and repeating a bunch of words without any feeling or comprehension isn't a true heartfelt response. It doesn't matter what you say if you don't mean the things you are saying. It's about being real and telling God where you're at and asking Him to take control of your life and open your heart up to it. It's also about being honest that you don't really understand a lot of it, but you're willing to genuinely seek it out.

There was some head nodding as well as confused looks as I spoke. I didn't use a ton of fancy words and stuff they wouldn't understand, I spoke naturally. I also didn't use some formulaic prayer or specific words, but I did point them to some passages in the Bible as to what's been spoken. All of that led to more questions about the Bible, "Can we trust it?" "Is it real?"

But maybe the most meaningful part to our conversation was near the end of it when Luke said, "OK, but I know a lot of Mormons and other people who think their religion is right."

I told him, "It's harsh and tough to tell someone they are wrong. I am not God, I don't want to be God, He is the one that judges. My role in life isn't to say who does and doesn't get into heaven. My role is to show the love Christ showed to others and spread His message of love to everyone that I can. Being a youth pastor wasn't my plan all along, I wanted to play baseball and be in a boy band (which got a good laugh), but God's message of love for this world was too hard for me to pass up. I needed to share that and be part of what He was doing in the world. I also needed to seek it out for myself and live it, rather than just go off of what someone had told me, even if that was my parents or someone I trusted."

I got a decent response to that, but felt they weren't quite buying it, which was fine, I wasn't trying to "convert" them in that moment. I only wanted to open their hearts up to what was really stirring in them, then let the Holy Spirit do the rest.

The last thing that I told them was this,

> *When I was younger, I always wanted to live in the 1950s. I wanted to come back in my next life as a kid in the 1950s. It just seemed like such a simple time and my plan was to buy a bunch of baseball cards so I could make money on them in the future, like a time machine I guess. I pictured myself the exact same way with the same people around me just like my current life. But no matter how much I wished and hoped something like that would come true*

after I die, the reality is that it won't, but something will. The truths I've learned in life are that, one, we all die, and two, something happens after we die. No matter how much I would love to make up what that looks like for my own life in the after-life, I can't. I have as little control over that as I did being brought into this world in the first place. So my goal in life is to find out what actually does happen after I die. And when I heard about heaven and dug deep into what God's promise through Jesus is, it sounded a lot more exciting and also realistic than me making up my own future plans. There has to be a universal truth out there, and not just one that "works" for me however I'd like it to. Our lives are too important and meaningful to chance it with a guessing game of "Choose your own adventure." And I've found that truth in the world to be Jesus Christ. I realized that I can't choose my options, but I have the option to choose one that's there already. Does that make sense?

"Yeah," Pete said. "I hadn't looked at things like that before, woah."

When we were done talking, I said, "Let's do this guys, for the next five weeks we're going to be studying a book on youth group nights here, it's all about wrestling with the questions that you're facing and digging for some answers. Will you guys come and be a part of that for the next five weeks?"

"I'll be there," Tyler said. "I'm down," both Luke and Pete said while nodding their heads in unison.

"Cool, then I'll see you guys next week. But hey, call me or drop by anytime if you want to chat some more. I love your questions and want to hear more about what's going on in your lives."

"Alright, peace out. Later," they all said while getting into their car and driving away. About one minute after they left, Tyler, who had brought them by and showed a tougher exterior while we were together, texted me saying "THX ☺" That kid was such a softy with a heart of gold and I loved it. He had no idea that he was such a gifted little evangelist.

It was awesome to see these guys questioning, because when you ask questions you find answers. This is what I loved the most about my job. I loved to teach, but I loved even more to see students grapple with deep questions about life and faith. It was so rewarding to be a part of that. I wasn't sure where all of it would end up leading in their lives, but the fact that they were seeking was a great thing. In fact, we had a pretty amazing group of students who were finding a fire for God. They weren't only participating in our programs at church, but really becoming advocates for it! Any youth group program that is based solely on one person's heart and vision will eventually crumble, but we had leaders with hearts full of passionate love for students and students that were falling in love with God and wanting everyone to know it.

The next week at youth group was incredible. Tyler, Luke and Pete all showed up, early even with some of their friends. Some of our other students who hadn't come consistently showed up as well as our regulars. I'd say there were over seventy-five students there that night. I was excited and a little nervous, questioning if my lesson and plan for the night was good enough or would be relevant to any of them. This was a common thought however, but with the amount of kids there, it was escalated.

I spent some time mingling through the parking lot, meeting new kids, chatting with the ones I already knew, and sharing a well-placed movie quote whenever the opportunity arose. One of my goals was to always be sure to make intentional contact with every student that came to church. This was a bit easier when ten kids were showing up, but that's why we had leaders, so we could fan out and show love and attention to all the students. Nothing is better than to let a student know that you have time for them and that you are singling them out, especially in a large crowd.

The scene was awesome. Kids were skateboarding, a few were not so discreetly smoking in their cars, wanting to be inconspicuous, while desperately hoping others would see them. Those were the kids that would make it even more obvious by dousing themselves with cologne or perfume and then stepping uncomfortably close to others only so they could smell it on their breath. Had to love the naivety on some level though, and I loved them all the same for it. The scene looked much more like a rock concert. It was the middle of winter so the temperature had fallen to a very bitter 62 degrees. It was also pitch black outside since it got dark that time of year at about 4:30 p.m.

It took a small army to get all of those kids herded up and into the youth room, and was even more difficult to find everyone a spot to sit. We ran out of chairs that night, but kids were cool with lying on the floor and leaning against walls. In youth ministry, that is the kind of problem that you pray for! As soon as everyone was settled in, we got going. We started as usual with a couple of games and skits. The skit that night involved two volunteers repeating a scene over and over where one would chug a bottle of Gatorade and the other would cram two Twinkies into their mouth as they hopped in and out of a time machine. It got messy and was hilarious, which I'm sure calmed the nerves of some of the students who were new as well as those who weren't.

The teaching time that night went well. As often happens in that kind of dynamic, you are pulled off track, either by a question or comment that leads to a tangent. But I was so open to that and really feel that's where ministry happens most. There was also a social dynamic that was being dealt with that night. As with every time you get a group of students or people together for that matter, there is that sense of competition, judgment and comparison that I wish we could just get rid of, but unfortunately it's present. There were the kids who were excited to see new faces and welcome them in, then there were the kids who were shy and didn't speak up because their comfort zones were compromised. And finally there were the kids who took a lot of ownership with their group and didn't like what they saw and didn't think those were good enough "church kids." That was one of my biggest pet peeves, which I was trying hard to dispel and change perspectives on. I've always asked what is a "church person" or "church type?" Is that what it's about? I stand firm that I've never met one person who hasn't been a "church type," since my definition of that would be someone who was sinful, broken, hurting, lost and seeking direction and meaning. That would pretty much sum up the entire human race.

The night was wrapping up and we prayed. I encouraged our prayers to be authentic and from the heart, so I challenged the students to not start with the typical "God, thank you for bringing us all here tonight." Not that it wasn't a good thing to pray, but because it's just a conditioned prayer that most kids will say because they don't know what else to say. I just wanted them to be real and say what was on their hearts.

That night after youth group, I headed to Chili's with a few leaders and students to talk more about our lives. It was like a floodgate of conversation was opening all around us. I felt like this was a conversation that started a long time ago and has been spoken throughout history and now, this was our time to be involved in it. Life seemed to feel right when truth and meaning were being explored.

For the next couple of weeks, we continued to grow our group. My vision of packing the youth room out so we'd force the church to build us a bigger space was starting to come true. Kids were stopping by church and I was out in the community and heading to the school on a regular basis. There was this buzz that in all of my years in ministry, both as a student and teacher, I'd never seen or felt before. Tyler, Luke and Pete kept stopping by, with Tyler being the most consistent. It was so good to see that this was all a priority for them, and I had become really close to a bunch of the students, especially Tyler. JoHanna and I had even had him over for dinner a few times. I was finally at a point where my marriage felt solid again, I was being used, and I felt the church was becoming trusting and confident in what they saw in me.

12

Cigarette in One Hand,
A Bible in the Other

"The living Jesus is a problem in our religious
institutions. Yes. Because if you are having a
funeral, a nice funeral, and the dead person starts
to move, there goes the funeral! And, dear brothers
and sisters, Jesus is moving!"
– Juan Carlos Ortiz, *Cry of the Human Heart*

Things were indeed going well, and I was ready for the reception of the booming youth group from the staff and parents. I knew that it wasn't about me; however, there was no denying the goodness and excitement that seemed to be taking our church and community by storm. This is why I felt excited and eager to talk to people when they would bring it up. Such was the case one day that week when I ran into a parent at the mall, who I didn't know very well. We recognized each other as I said a friendly hello and she smiled and waved as we passed. But as I kept walking, she turned and followed me with anticipation. She was an older lady who was a single mom and was new to the church. Her son had been attending our youth group for awhile, and ironically was the reason his mom started attending there too. I say ironically because here's what happened.

When I noticed her trying to get my attention, I stopped and asked her, "What's up?" in a casual tone. She responded back to me with a tone that was more concerning, "Well, I'm more than a little worried about how youth group is going." I was thinking to myself, what could the worry be? Most people loved to gauge groups on a numbers count, and even if I didn't, the numbers definitely showed that something good was happening.

So I asked, genuinely curious, "Worried? How come? Things are going really well."

She said, "Well, I heard from another parent that there were some kids smoking in the parking lot the other night."

Not that this wasn't a legit concern, but again, something like this always seemed to be the bigger topic. Smoking in the parking lot was a bigger deal than the kids whose lives were being changed by their encounters with Jesus. And I wanted to respond back with "Well, at least they're at church. The kids are smoking with one hand and have a Bible in the other! Yeah! We got the party crowd kids reading the Bible! Awesome!"

Those are all of the things I was thinking, but didn't say. The rest of the conversation was me apologizing, telling her what she wanted to hear, promising I would be more like a police officer than a youth pastor and sending her off knowing that this "problem" would be taken care of and that her son wouldn't be corrupted at church. I always left those types of conversations sad. I was sad that I felt compelled to justify everything, I was sad that people couldn't look past the outward to see what was going on inside, and I was sad that the thinking didn't go past a cigarette. I wanted the opportunity to share the moment I'd had with Tyler at camp, and I wanted the chance to tell people what was really going on within the youth program. But the truth was, for the most part, the comfort zone of a comfortable church was compromised, and when that happens, the real ministry is overshadowed.

I had a similar conversation with a staff person later that week. We were walking outside together, down to a storage shed, and he told me as we walked past the stairs and railings that there were a bunch of high school kids there the other night skateboarding. Simultaneously we spoke, and as I said, "That's awesome!" he said, "It's a problem." We both stopped and looked at each other as it got awkward. He explained that it vandalized the property and church and made skid marks on the concrete. I admit, I laughed immaturely at the term "skid marks." It was just kind of the way he said it. I'm not a fan of vandalism, so I understood that. But again, I'm thinking, at least kids are hanging out at church! The very next week there were signs all around our church campus barricading every possible zone for a skateboarder with the words "NO SKATEBOARDING HERE, YOU WILL BE ARRESTED AND PROSECUTED." Harsh, right? I was thinking; these are kids, not terrorists. They aren't tagging our building and purposely being destructive, they are just looking for a place to be and play. And by putting up signs like that, the only message that kids were going to hear was "You are NOT welcome here." It broke my heart. If kids weren't smoking in the parking lot of church or skating on the stairs of them, they'd just find somewhere else to do it. Here they were loved and finding a deeper meaning for their lives.

I left church that day feeling discouraged, the ever consistent roller coaster feelings consumed me. While I was on my way home, I stopped by a park to grab a soda out of the machine. Almost immediately after my foot hit the ground to get out of the car, my cell phone rang. It was a Minnesota number, which was always interesting, and it wasn't programmed into my phone, which made it more interesting because I would always wonder who it was. Maybe I should've changed my cell phone to a California number, but, I hadn't gotten around to it yet. Regardless, I answered the phone with anticipation.

"Hello?"

It was my brother-in-law, Shawn (whom I really liked, but hadn't gotten to spend much time with, and also had never received a phone call from). The first thing he asked me was, "Is JoHanna with you?" Confused, I said, "No." He said, "Well, we wanted to call to let you know that her dad just had a stroke. It was a freak thing out of nowhere, and he was airlifted to the hospital this afternoon. He was conscious enough to call 911 and when they got to the house, he was found in the driver's seat of his car that had backed through the garage door. Apparently he was leaving to go back to work after lunch and it just happened. It doesn't look good right now and we thought that you should be with JoHanna when she finds out."

I had already jumped back into my car at this point and was about five minutes from home. The only things that I could really ask were, "How is everyone else?" "How did this happen?" "What is going to happen?" Many questions that there were obviously no answers to, but in a moment like that, that's your reality.

We hung up pretty quickly. I tried to gather my thoughts as I briskly walked into our apartment. I found JoHanna hanging out in the kitchen putting some dishes away. She was smiling and in a really good mood. I feel like that is always when those kinds of things hit.

I sat her down in the living room and without any real preparations or much time to even process myself, I spoke.

"Your dad was in an accident."

Followed immediately by, "But he's still alive."

"Wait, what are you talking about?!" she responded frantically.

"Shawn called and he told me that your dad suffered a stroke."

I told her the only details I knew and that I'd start looking for flights online so we could get back there. She was concerned and shocked, but her immediate reaction was frustration that her family didn't call her themselves. They had called me, which to be honest was the right way to do it. Not that there was an easy way, but I think we both agreed on it deep down.

I held her for awhile on the oversized papasan chair in our living room, as she obsessively kept trying to call her mom. Her mom finally picked up and they talked for awhile. I stood in the room as they spoke, and she seemed to come out of the conversation a little less frustrated, but worried all the same. There were many unanswered questions and future unknowns. After a few hours we decided the best thing to do was to have JoHanna fly up there for a few days to spend some time with everyone, and I'd be available to fly up as needed. She was prepared to leave the next day. It worked out since she still didn't have a job and had barely been temping week to week. And at that time her dad needed to go through a couple of very serious brain surgeries within the next few hours. It was also a big concern to see if he would even live through the surgeries. There was a lot of worry and prayer happening in our lives that day.

Carrying a burden of unanswered questions is tough, it's even more difficult to try and pray the prayer of "your will be done," because selfishly we always want the person who is sick to be healed. I spoke about all of this to a pastor that I trusted. He told me some words that helped put things into perspective a little better from God's point of view. He said, "Look at it this way, either way he's going to be healed, right?" That was true, and just the way he said those words offered a lot of hope and comfort. It was a confident faith talking, not a cop-out or insincere rambling. Even though we weren't sure of the long-term effects, God was, He was in control of it. That was the comfort that we took, and while we were praying for healing, the reality of ultimate healing was sinking in. It didn't drown out much of the anxious frustration that we felt, but at least for JoHanna and me, it offered a sense of peace.

Later that night, we found out that the initial surgeries were as successful as they could be and the doctors were optimistic that a recovery of some kind would be possible. There was no time table set, but we at least had that to encourage us as I said goodbye to JoHanna at the airport the next day as she headed back to Minnesota. No matter what was going to happen, it was clear that her father was a beautiful story of redemption that could've rivaled many biblical characters. He was clearly a man used by God and whose life had been transformed by the power of God's goodness. He had surrendered to that and had become a man after God's own heart. He was a great testimony to the life transformation that God gives, as well as the fragileness of it all, considering that he was a healthy, active, forty-nine-year-old man. I couldn't help but be in awe of the power of God working, yet was still struggling with the tough circumstances. My mind was trying to comprehend what my heart was dealing with.

I threw a small party for myself after JoHanna left. Not the kind that you're probably picturing in your head however. It was a great pity party, filled with questioning and bitterness. My emotions started to take a toll. Just when I felt that things were going so awesome, not only was I confronted in a couple of conversations that blatantly disregarded the goodness of what was going on in the youth group, but JoHanna's father, my father-in-law, was fighting for his life. And as much as I kept reminding myself that this was all God's plan, I started questioning it more than I ever had. But, I pressed on, knowing there was a vision set out before me still and a meaning for everything, and I reminded myself after a few days of grappling, that it wasn't about me. Although I was having a tough time, I turned to the good that was going on. And for that I didn't need to look too far, as I found myself on the school campus the next day.

13

Comfort Zones Compromised

"We think sometimes that poverty is only being
hungry, naked and homeless. The poverty of being
unwanted, unloved and uncared for is the greatest
poverty."
– Mother Teresa

There was a different vibe around the high school than when I first started visiting there. Not only was I gaining some respect, I was actually getting to know a lot of the teachers too. And instead of putting myself on the line trying to talk to students, enough of them knew me where I didn't have to approach any of them, I'd let them come to me. This was good and bad, because I knew there was more work to do, but if I could have painted a picture of what that school looked like and the buzz that surrounded it that winter and spring, it wouldn't look close to what it was the previous fall. The Holy Spirit had a grip on that place and our students were being Jesus with skin on every day. And others noticed it also, as teachers would confirm it to me. I even got asked to speak over lunchtime at the Christian Club on campus that students from my church had started! If ever I needed encouragement to do what I was doing, all I had to do was look at the faces of the students reaching out in their school and look into the eyes of those they were reaching for.

Before I left campus that day, I had met up with Tyler for a minute and he said he'd stop by church after school.

When coming to faith and developing your Christian walk, something that's tough to do sometimes is to figure out exactly what God wants specifically out of each of us. It's like we have the believing thing down, but then it's the "Now what?" It's hard when we see so many rough things going on in the world to feel as though we matter or that we can ultimately make any sort of significant difference. And that can get very frustrating. But that's why God has gifted each person with different strengths and abilities and different hearts for specific things. And crazy things can happen when we figure that out and surrender to it. When it all fits and makes sense, it can also make you do crazy things. Like when you fall in love with teaching and mentoring high school kids, you may, for example, up and leave everything you know to move from Minnesota to California.

This was the essence of a conversation that I had with Tyler. He was struggling to figure out how to live and what to do now after he had been gaining so much knowledge and passion within his relationship with God. He was very honest in telling me, "Yeah, I don't really like kids, they annoy me." So, I assumed leading a VBS program for kids probably wouldn't be a good fit. I asked him, "What's something that just breaks your heart?" He wasn't really sure. I told him, "Well, there is something and when you figure that out, that's what your calling is. It will be connected to an opportunity and all of your strengths and gifts which you already have." That is ministry. And I reminded him that being a Christian really was to be "Christ-like," and acting as the person of Christ, with all the gifts of the spirit; love, joy, peace, patience, kindness, goodness, faithfulness, gentleness and self-control. I told him that we are saved by grace alone, not by our works, and in the Bible it says, "For it is by grace you have been saved, through faith—and this not from yourselves, it is the gift of God—not by works, so that no one can boast. For we are God's workmanship, created in Christ Jesus to do good works, which God prepared in advance for us to do," (Eph. 2:8-9). We are saved BY grace FOR good works, not saved by our good works. I said, "Remember at camp when I shared the example about giving jewelry to my wife? That I wanted to do it because I loved her, not because I was supposed to or had to? Because once we enter into that relationship, there's work to be done!"

This all seemed to make sense to him. I reassured him that he'd find what he was looking for, even if he didn't know what that was yet, but I couldn't wait to see what would happen when he did. And his purpose could be found in whatever profession he chose or wherever he went in life, he just needed to be faithful in it. This was all so new to him that his honesty and eagerness were very contagious. And coming up, there was a very timely opportunity for us to serve as a youth group and I really wanted Tyler to be a part of it.

With the help of a couple of other leaders, I had been planning and organizing a youth service event in Downtown Los Angeles at a Rescue Mission. I wanted to make sure this was a youth group that wasn't just about learning and hanging out, but that we were equipped and excited about going out and *doing* as well. And *doing* outside of our church and immediate comfort zones too.

The outward actions show the inward heart.

I really believe strongly in that. It's what I had been talking to Tyler about. It's one thing to know and feel something, but it's another to act on that love and faith.

Jesus says this in Matthew 25:35-40,

> *For I was hungry and you gave me something to eat, I was thirsty and you gave me something to drink, I was a stranger and you invited me in, I needed clothes and you clothed me, I was sick and you looked after me, I was in prison and you came to visit me.' "Then the righteous will answer him, 'Lord, when did we see you hungry and feed you, or thirsty and give you something to drink? When did we see you a stranger and invite you in, or needing clothes and clothe you? When did we see you sick or in prison and go to visit you? The King will reply, 'I tell you the truth, whatever you did for one of the least of these brothers of mine, you did for me.'*

Jesus doesn't talk about serving as a way of feeling bad. Yeah, that's part of it, but compassion is a verb. It's an action. This passage says "I was hungry and you *gave me,* a stranger and you *invited* me, in prison and you *visited* me; etc." These are all actions and examples of *showing* compassion, and not just feeling bummed out about it. It doesn't say, I was hungry and needed clothes, and you felt really bad for me. Loving and Compassion are action words. Actually, **when we let love win, that's when compassion happens.**

—∿—

I got Tyler to sign-up for this day trip so he could try it out. He'd never done anything like this before. Our community was kind of a bubble and until you ventured outside of it, it was pretty easy to stay safe and confined into a comfortable life, which is how many people lived. Seeing someone who was homeless was rare, unless you saw the man that always sat on the median from the off ramp to one of the major exits in our town.

I knew there were students who were very excited about the opportunity to go downtown and they'd been talking about it for weeks, but kids tend to not plan very far ahead, so by Friday night, the day before we left, there were six kids signed up. That was fine, but a far cry from the number of students who were now calling our church their home and our group their group. I was thinking that night that we'd only be going with six, which would mean we could all fit into two vehicles, or easily all into the church van. Church van trips were always interesting. So, I coordinated and planned accordingly, but like usual, plans changed.

By the time I fell asleep that night, I had gotten three texts and two phone calls from five different kids that wanted to join in on what we were doing. By the early morning (we were meeting at 9 a.m.), I had a few more phone calls and then some more kids just started showing up in the parking lot. Before long, our group of six had swelled to twenty-four. I was frantically calling everyone I knew to help drive. By the time we were pulling out of the parking lot, it was almost an hour after we had planned to leave, and we had a caravan of five SUVs and vans going, including one driven by our senior pastor who I'd woken up to join in on the event.

I called the rescue mission on our way to give them the heads up on our change in numbers and also used the traffic excuse, which I found holds a lot of weight in Southern California, as a result I found myself using it often. We raced down the freeway, trying to keep pace with each other in the caravan. There were competitions going on between cars, like when the kids would be singing a Kelly Clarkson song at the top of their lungs and dancing in one van, assuming that everyone else could hear every word. My car was doing the exact same thing; but substituting Aaron Carter for Kelly Clarkson. Those are always good memories to make and keep. I couldn't help but think of how awesome it was to have a group of high school kids who got up on a beautiful Saturday morning to go serve meals to the less fortunate in downtown Los Angeles, with nothing to receive in return. It was a feat in itself that they were even up at that hour. Again: High school kids aren't given enough credit. These kids were an example of that. And throughout the day, I didn't hear a single complaint out of one of their mouths. They served with a sense of joy which was an example to everyone.

As we approached the rescue mission, there were a few blocks that were pretty disturbing to see. The comforts that we all knew from a safe and loving community looked to be lost in these streets. The blocks were filled with garbage, broken store windows, barbed wire and boarded up shops. But more heart-wrenching was the look of despair and lack of hope on many faces of the people that filled the streets and sidewalks in that lost district of humanity. It felt like the world had given up on them and they had come to accept that. At least that is the impression you got when looking into those people's eyes while driving through the streets. We turned down into a guarded and gated parking ramp and went underground. When we got out of the cars, the demeanor of the students had changed. There wasn't any more dancing, just the look of hurt and shock, which was mixed with looks of optimism, compassion and love. It was a sense of, what can we do? And that immediate response translated throughout the day.

As we got into the building we were greeted by warm faces in the volunteer department, which was a small cramped space, as well as welcoming smiles from the residents there. We met up with our coordinator Randy, and were led straight into the kitchen. The students all stood in line as they got decked out in their proper kitchen attire; complete with lovely hairnets and plastic aprons. It was sweet.

Everyone listened as one of the residents there, who also ran the kitchen, explained what was going to happen and started dividing everyone up into their jobs. There were two things I saw come out of that. One thing was that the kids were almost fighting with each other for the different opportunities, whether it was to serve the food, or prepare it in the back. They wanted to do it all! And the second thing was the respect and attention they gave the man in the kitchen. I was hoping to take him back to the church with us to be my attention getter.

We worked hard and met a lot of people coming in to eat. We were able to share a few stories and interact as well. We had a great time serving, and at about 2:00 p.m., it was our turn to eat. We all dished up our meals and sat in the cafeteria. While we ate, the president of the mission came and spoke to our group. That was very cool. He talked about homelessness and how a person becomes homeless and what they do at the mission etc. He also answered a lot of questions the kids had. After that, he led us all on a tour of the building and facilities. The kids really liked it and it gave them a good sense of the reality of how far too many people live. I could see the kids getting a sense of what the world looks like outside of their own bubble of safety.

One of the picture snapshots I took away in my head from that day was when we were up on the rooftop of the six story building and the kids were just looking over the edge in awe. They were staring over blocks and blocks of garbage, bodies and waste. Quite honestly it looked like a human dumping ground. I kept getting the image of Jesus walking through the streets hanging out with those people. He definitely wouldn't come to our community first when He came back; there was just too much hurt and despair in places like this. Their biggest worries weren't over what got erased on Tivo and who was going to the party, no, they wondered if they were going to make it through the night without getting robbed, beaten up or worse.

The kids all stood in silence as I stood by a couple of the leaders doing the same thing. But it all becomes much more realistic when you add the smells, sounds and atmosphere that you can't get in your living room from the TV. After we finally started to gather back toward the elevator, I noticed that Tyler hadn't moved. I walked over to help encourage him to keep moving. And while I was approaching him I was thinking about how he hadn't said much all day. I had the sense that he was out of it and didn't care at all. Just like camp, I kept thinking that he didn't want to be there, even though he had told me he'd try it out. He didn't say anything to me as we walked away from the wall and then eventually back out to the cars to head home. Maybe this wasn't his thing either. He was starting to live a life like Christ, but struggling even more to find out what that looked like, and when there's nothing that breaks your heart, it's hard to be someone passionate about serving others. In fact, that day overall he had looked disinterested and tired.

When we got back to church, we had a brief time of prayer and the kids were very excited about what the day had held, but more so about what the future would hold. "Can we go back there every month?" someone asked me. And then immediately following that comment, someone else said, to a rousing cheer from the rest, "No, every *week*!" These students were amazing. I was so proud of each of them. As we visioned in the parking lot for a few minutes over what we could do as a large group, I noticed Tyler's car flying out of the parking lot at the other end of the church. Maybe this day had been a waste of his time.

14

The Gospel According to YOU

"Men read and admire the gospel of Christ,
With its love so unfailing and true;
But what do they say, and what do they think
Of the gospel according to you?

You are writing each day a letter to men;
Take care that the writing is true.
'Tis the only gospel some men will read,
That gospel according to you."
– Author Unknown

I saw a lot of the kids who went to the Mission with us the following day at church. Many of them had started coming to our latest and most contemporary service. I'm not sure if it was because they loved the service so much, or they felt comfortable there and wanted to come and connect with each other. Either way was good with me! It felt nice to see all of their faces on the church grounds on a Sunday morning. I'd even heard some of the kids say that it was a priority for them. That was pretty great. We did have a teaching time on Sunday morning as well. I don't like the term "Sunday school," but basically that's what it was. It was for about half an hour and most of the kids would skip the church part, and hang over in the youth room until we met. It would have been cool to have gotten them all into the sanctuary where we started out, but with students who haven't ever attended church or who've had a bad experience with church, you take what you can get and work towards helping them fall in love with God, not just filling a pew.

I have a tendency to tell pretty awful jokes, which in turn makes things awkward and ultimately gets a better laugh, and since I am so comfortable with self-deprecating humor, I relished it. I shared a joke that morning; it's an old one I heard growing up. I asked the kids "You know what they say about the guy that farts in church don't you? ... pause. Well he sits in his own pew!" I smiled to no reaction and only crickets. There was a sympathy giggle or two, but mostly dead air. High school kids are nothing if not honest. It occurred to me immediately after I said that, that kids might not even know what pews are, I think that's kind of old school. Here were some other responses, "Dude, worst joke ever," "Huh? I don't even get it." "Way lame." And the list goes on. To be honest, those were the moments I cherished the most. It was those little things that were the building blocks that built the bigger relational stuff.

I spent most of the time that morning talking about the rescue mission experience and letting kids reflect on it. It's always so good to debrief those types of things, whether it's on a large or small scale. Students need an opportunity to process their thoughts and feelings and correlate it to their spiritual life and faith. A lot of kids talked about how guilty or selfish they felt. I appreciated their responses and feelings, but that wasn't the intent or point, to make ourselves feel crappy for living where we do and how we do. The key was to figure out what we're called to do and how we're supposed to treat those who don't have some of the advantages that we have. And to live sacrificial lives that extended past our own individual bubble worlds, and to see in other people, what they have that *we* are lacking.

There were some good thoughts and great perspectives given. A lot of students were trying to figure out how we could reach out in our own community and how they could do it by themselves to start a revolution. I shared a story about a high school kid who was very disturbed to hear that there are still about twenty-seven million modern day slaves in the world. He started collecting change and would actually buy people out of slavery. It grew into a huge ministry. I wanted the kids to think big like that, but not feel like they had to help everyone. It was like what I had been talking to Tyler about. Find something you're passionate about and good at, then find a need and fill it. This is what ministry looks like. It could be starting a huge orphanage in Africa, or it could be bringing a meal to a person in the community who can't leave their home. No matter how big or small, we are all expected to do that in many different ways.

I wanted them to not feel like if they couldn't change everything or save the world, why try? The main thing was to walk consistently with a vision of Jesus and to treat everyone how He would've. And it wasn't because I was saying it or telling them, I told them to read it for themselves in the Bible.

The last thing we talked about was how our lives need to look different than those around us. We are as the Bible says in 1 Peter 2:11, "aliens and strangers in this world." Jesus looked different from the world when He walked it, and that's what we should do also. We need to live lives that make people question and demand an explanation. And there's a lot of risk involved in that, it's not easy. Each of us has a story to live out and with its uniqueness and struggles we're no different than any of the people who met God throughout the Bible. I asked them, "What would the gospel according to YOU, look like? The gospels were all accounts of Jesus' life and the stories in the Bible were about real people meeting Christ, struggling with faith and rising up with God's strength. It's about a God of love who became a man to show love to His people. What would you write? What would be written about you? There's not one person who has a story even close to your own, which means God is telling His story through you. The world needs to hear it! Because **your life might be the only Bible that someone reads**."

I wanted kids to know that their lives were significant. And not because I thought so, which I did, but because God thinks so! When I was done, I felt an undeniable energy in the room. I told the kids that we were all going to start telling our stories to each other. At our weekly youth group I was going to start having one student each week get up and tell us about their life, passions, heart and who God is in their lives and their own personal experiences with Him. I painted it in a more exciting way than just saying, "We will be sharing our testimonies." That scares people away sometimes because they don't quite know what it means, or don't think their story is worthy of a "testimony."

I asked for a volunteer who wanted to kick us off that week. As much of a buzz there was in the room, there was tumbleweed rolling past when I asked that. But then I looked in the back of the room, and one hand shot up like a bottle rocket with the bold and confident words, "I'm down. I got this." It was Tyler. Of course it was. I felt the excitement rush back into the room. All of the students started whispering and were almost giddy to hear what he would have to say, because even though some of them had known him forever, they were now seeing the change in his life, even those who were skeptical. I felt like one of the students at that moment, with all of the same exact feelings. I couldn't wait to hear what he'd have to share!

15

Story-Telling

"No, life cannot be understood flat on a page. It has to be lived; a person has to get out of his head, has to fall in love, has to memorize poems, has to jump off bridges into rivers, has to stand in an empty desert and whisper sonnets under his breath... We get one story, you and I, and one story alone. God has established the elements, the setting and the climax and resolution. It would be a crime not to venture out, wouldn't it?"

– Donald Miller, *Through Painted Deserts*

The next day I had a date with my wife with a few friends we had made. We were looking forward to going out to eat, since that wasn't something we were able to do very often due to the enormous paychecks I was raking in. And that was all right with us, but we definitely didn't take going out to eat for granted. We met up with two other couples who were about our same age. One of the couples we'd met loosely through a family at my church and the other couple were friends of theirs who we'd gotten to like very well. It was something that we probably built up too much in our heads, at least I know I did because I missed all of my friends back home so much. I had idealized finding the perfect friend situation in California, and wanted it to look like the show *Friends*. Naturally, I would play Chandler because of my humor and inappropriateness in uncomfortable situations. I figured however, that this was a lot of pressure to put on everyone else in our own little group, I mean who would play the rest of the cast?

Alas, it never really looked like the show *Friends,* but it was a nice group of people none-the-less. Having the chance to hang out with people, who were for the most part outsiders of the church, gave me a chance to wear a different hat. You're asked to wear many different hats when you are in ministry, and at times they are justified, but other times they can become uncomfortable. I realized that no matter what you did or how you acted, people always seemed to have a perception of who you are, and what you're supposed to be and do. And sometimes it seemed as though certain people would have a pen and pad in their hands waiting to demark you once they saw you step out of the realm of their own expectations.

Now, I know I'm not perfect. I understand and accept that while striving to be a person of integrity. But sometimes, I find myself wondering and even laughing inside when I think, "Man, if they only knew what I was thinking…" And this all had nothing to do with a hypocritical lifestyle; I like to think that I live a pretty consistent life in every area and aspect, but also have many flaws and enjoy living a life outside of the box of others' expectations.

Unfortunately I often catch myself spending too much time looking over my shoulder, for no apparent reason.

All that to say that this group was becoming a transplant of what I'd had in Minnesota. We sat down for dinner that night and ordered a couple pitchers of beer, a plate of appetizers, which I thought looked more like a heart attack platter, and some of the best chips and salsa that I'd ever eaten. We spent the night talking. We discussed life, talked about ourselves, listened to each other and shared embarrassing stories. It was three of the best hours I can remember spending within recent memory.

—⋙—

Later that week, Tyler called me. It was the night before youth group and he had been preparing his talk. It was so cool to hear how serious he was taking it. The first thing he said to me, which was very innocent, was, "Am I doing this right?" I didn't like hearing kids think there was a right or wrong way to tell their story.

I told him, "Whatever you talk about is 'right.' It's your life, it's your own story, and there's no wrong way to tell it!"

I could tell he was a little nervous about what to say, and how much he could say. Although he was confident by nature, this was a huge step for him. A step he needed to go through to put his whole life into perspective, if only for himself. It just so happened that he would be sharing it with his peers.

I told him, "Just keep it real. Tell about your life, your experiences, your encounter with God, what life changes have taken place, how your past has shaped who you are, and how Christ has now also shaped who you are. Who's the old you? Who's the current you? Who's the Tyler that will be in the future?" I guess I sounded a little too cliché and go get 'em. The truth is that I only wanted him to be real. Too many people stress over finding the best things to say, and want to embellish their stories to make them more thrilling or exciting, kind of like a Hollywood script.

I had shared plenty of my own personal stories and struggles with Tyler in the past, and I reminded him of those. I also had a very hard time when I would get an opportunity to share about my life, because I didn't think it was exciting. I went through some trials and had plenty of times where I saw God at work, but it wasn't ever as exciting as hearing other people tell about themselves. I never had a huge "Come to Christ" moment. My life and faith walk had been more gradual. But then at one point in my life my mom told me that my faith story consisted more of what God had kept me from, rather than what He's pulled me out of.

I felt more comfortable hearing that. The coolest thing about a life story and testimony is that it is an ongoing process. God sees us through all of our trials and triumphs while life is continually changing around us. I always think it's funny when people ask, "When were you saved?" I tend to give a sarcastic answer and say, "Well, not exactly sure, but it was some Friday over 2,000 years ago!" I usually get a confused, uncomfortable smile after that. Because to me, which I'd talked with Tyler about, being a Christian is an every day thing. To be like Christ is to walk like Him every day and make a conscious choice to do that. I don't think I lose my salvation when I slip up, that's where God's grace comes in, but I also don't look at it as, "I've punched my ticket, now I can live life however the heck I want to." The gift of salvation is much too important and precious to not give everything I have in response to it.

I think Tyler calmed himself down. He just wanted to work things out in his own mind, and nothing I said probably penetrated his thought process or would change his delivery, but I loved watching God work in his life. I couldn't wait until the next night to hear what Tyler was going to say. It was one thing to be watching his life transformation, but quite another to get the chance to really hear him articulate it.

I was stoked to be at church the following night. I felt like a participant and not the leader. I was just the warm-up for the main act. I was pretty sure most of the kids didn't even remember we were starting our story sharing time that night. It didn't matter though, I knew Tyler was ready and I knew the kids would respond well, which they did. When I got up front to do a few announcements, I reminded them all that we were starting our story sharing, and Tyler was going to speak first that night. That sparked more smiles and whispers. The room was packed. We were consistently growing and new faces were showing up every week, but there was some extra buzz in the room at that point because I'd say at least fifteen of the students were friends of Tyler's who starting coming because he'd invited them. They were genuinely searching and seeking and had pretty tough exteriors. They were widely known as the crazy party crowd, but you could tell they were respectful as well. Those were the kids you wanted at church!

When we had finished making our usual mess with games and gotten through a worship set, I invited Tyler to come up front. He popped right up and jogged to the stage. I also noticed he wasn't carrying notes or anything. He stood up front with a confident look and had his hands in his pockets that reminded me he was still shy and nervous, but eager to talk.

His story started from the beginning. He talked about his life growing up, his family, his parents and brother. He spoke about his relationship with his brother, how their closeness was "like literally having a second brain." He focused on his achievements and his experience with the church. About how he'd known of Jesus and had some head knowledge, but never took it seriously. He said, "I never took faith seriously until the day my brother left the earth."

That drew the room in. The audience was captivated by his words, more so than I'd seen in a long time. Everyone had known about his brother, but it wasn't ever talked about. And for me personally, other than Tyler sharing about it with me at camp, I hadn't heard much more about it either. It was hard enough to hear about his relationship with his brother when he was alive, but then he spoke about his death.

"I guess that's when my faith really started, and by that I mean, I lost it and had none. I couldn't find myself believing in a God who would take away the closest person in my life when we were only fourteen years old. And nobody had any answers, and that's what I wanted. I started to feel like it was all a joke and B.S. and wanted nothing to do with God. I truly felt like nothing mattered and I didn't care about anything, man. All I kept doing at night was hoping I'd get a chance to go rafting or fishing and then picturing myself drowning to be out of this place."

He talked about his parents, their fighting, their own coping with Jacob's death and how they couldn't even look at him because he reminded them so much of Jacob. He felt guilty, ashamed and alone. So because of that, as a lot of people do, he turned to anything that would give him a sense of life, or something that would alter his reality. He talked about doing drugs, drinking and sleeping with girls. He talked about how his lifestyle looked and how even though he tried so much not to care, he always did and it made him feel worse.

"Every time I made a bad choice, I found myself questioning why I was doing it, and knew it wasn't OK. I knew there was more to life and would pray that if there really was a God, show me something real. I would pray to my brother and ask him to show me where he was and if there's really a heaven, what am I doing wrong here?"

Everyone was listening and seemed to be thinking about their own life and how it looked. You can have the biggest, most powerful evangelist speaker in the world come and speak to thousands of people, but that doesn't compete or even come close to when someone shares their most intimate story of faith and struggles in such a way that Tyler did that night. I was so amazed at his boldness and how he kept his composure speaking; nobody was concerned about the time that night, as if the clock on the wall didn't exist.

He spoke through all of this stuff, which even some of his best friends didn't know. At one point he smiled and said, "And then someone invited me out for buffalo wings. Evan. He kept bugging me to hang, even though I was a jerk to him. He took his stalking to creeper status." The room burst into laughter. "He even came to school and talked about the Backstreet Boys in front of my friends to get my attention."

The room laughed again. "He saw something in me, I guess, I mean I am pretty amazing… but seriously, I think he just wanted to see what God put in me. I've learned so much about God over the past few months. He's pretty sweet. He has made me unique and for a reason, and blessed me with so many things beyond belief. I realize that I don't need all of the answers to why things happen the way that they do. I guess that's what faith is. But I do know enough to know that I need to surrender my life to God and respond the only way I can, by following Jesus Christ for the rest of my life. A bunch of my friends always claim to have no faith, and say that there is no God. Guys, believing there is no God *is* a faith. A faith that there's nothing there. So what, we're born, live how we want, die and rot? Think about it. How awful is that? I can't go on believing that anymore."

It was a profound ending to a truly great story. It's why I love youth ministry. When he was finished, the room erupted with cheers. I came up and prayed and that led to a ton of hugs, tears and laughter. The whole night was spirit-led and I couldn't have been more proud of Tyler. He was one of the most courageous people I'd ever met in my life and as I was locking up that night, I saw him in the parking lot hanging with a group of his friends talking. I couldn't actually hear what they were talking about, but I knew. This was a kid with a story to tell and he was telling it in every aspect of his life, and it was contagious. I looked over at him and he smiled and pointed at me with that whole, "You, man" look. I fired a point right back as if I was saying, "Nah, YOU man."

I was happy.

I was happy with Tyler. I was so impressed by his willingness to share all of his personal stories with others. I knew I wouldn't have gone that far when I was his age. I would've wanted to, I would've shared some stuff, but I know that because of fear, rejection or vulnerability, I would have stopped at a certain point and not let on who I really was. And the hard thing was, those times would happen most when I was around the people who were closest to me. Why is that?

There seems to be something about that, in life, when our desire to share and open up sometimes gets stifled when it comes to those who are supposed to accept us the most. I'm thankful that I have gotten over a lot of that, but our insecurities always seem to know which buttons to push on our brain. The bottom line is that it's a tough thing to do. It takes courage and a gift. Tyler had the gift. I won't ever forget the image of him standing there talking with his friends in the parking lot. It appeared to be so innocent, but I knew the depths of what was being discussed.

The next couple of weeks a lot of students starting sharing life stories. There were students who I'd never really heard say much of anything other than "Dude" or "Nice," speaking their minds and hearts. They wanted to talk about personal struggles, seek advice and find someone to share their burdens. I would consider a lot of these the lost kids in the youth group. Not lost in the sense of they had no direction, but many would get lost in the shuffle, no matter how intentional we were at seeking out each individual kid. That's what made it so precious to hear them speak and be validated. Tyler's speaking made it OK to talk about what was *really* going on in their lives, and not just feeling as though it all had to be sugar coated. Tyler's message went much deeper than I had even realized.

One girl, Kara, actually came up to me and said, "This is the first time I have felt comfortable speaking to anyone about my problems, and for once in my life, I feel all right about who I am." Kara had been in the youth group for the past two years, but had never built up the trust or confidence to be able to share with anyone. She had really connected to Alexa, and because of that relationship, was able to become more whole through dealing with her circumstances and not just ignoring them. If God gives rest to the weary and broken, then our entire youth group was ready for a few months of hibernation. It's crazy how an encounter with Christ combined with people being real, can break so many down to be built up and truly start a revolution. I was personally learning so much from all of these kids.

It's hard to consider yourself a teacher when you are still constantly a student.

16

Tragedy Strikes

"I was … pondering what my life would have looked like if I didn't ever get into ministry. I thought about what if I was doing something wrong? I wondered if I could've saved him, and I wondered what the fastest highway out of California was, because I was ready to run away."
– Evan Gratz

JoHanna and I were spending a beautiful night at home. We had the windows open and were enjoying the distant ocean breezes. I had cooked dinner that Friday night, which was a rarity. I made my specialty; brats. They weren't just any kind of brats though. They were the ones with cheese in them. I broiled them which meant no matter how many holes you poked through them, most of the cheese would explode all over the oven sheet anyway. I would then throw the buns in the oven so they'd get nice and golden brown. I also brought out all of the amazing condiments including jalapenos, which I had started to put on everything since moving to California. To top it off, I made baked beans and broke open a bag of chips, sea salt and vinegar, which typically made their way onto the brats.

After dinner we sat down in the living room and started our movie night. Those regularly consisted of an animated movie that led into a comedy and ended with either a serious drama or suspenseful movie. The planning and expectations were always high for those low-key nights. However, whenever we tried to do a movie night, it ended up being more of a preview/clip night, with me sitting on the floor in front of the DVD player repeatedly flipping through all of our DVDs because nothing seemed good enough to watch. We'd start and stop probably five different movies on average those nights, but it was all good. We loved nights like that and looked forward to them. Things were so much better between us, and my father-in-law was in a slow, but promising recovery. We were intentional about letting that time be all about us, which is why we always made sure to turn our cell phones off. But for some reason, unfortunately and fortunately, that particular night I didn't.

I was laughing at something my wife had said while leaning up against the couch in our living room. The volume had been turned down on the TV and there was more conversation between us than movie watching at that point. I looked at JoHanna as she was reaching for her glass of water blindly. As she stretched her arm over the back of her head, around her neck and to the other side to grab it, she hit the lampshade, which in turn ricocheted off of the plant jar holding a dead cactus, and then knocked the entire glass of water all over. That seemed to happen at least once a week at our place, so it wasn't a big deal, especially since it was only water this time. She hopped up to grab a towel as I started damage control by removing all of the remotes and things that were in the path of the creeping stream and puddle of water that was on the end table now making a waterfall to the floor. As we settled back down into place, in which we thought at the time would be our biggest crisis of the evening, my phone rang, and it rang loudly! I thought I had turned it off, but instead I had accidentally turned the ringer on to violently loud. When my phone was on it was usually set to vibrate, so it took a second to figure out exactly what was happening as we were both startled by it.

It was Tyler calling and it was 9:30 at night. That wasn't too uncommon, because he'd call quite a bit, but something felt strange about the call that night. I was anxious as I picked up the phone while walking through our front door to the porch to get a little privacy and cell phone reception.

I picked it up, "Tyler? What's up my man?" eagerly awaiting a reply.

He said, "Hey man, not much, just driving with Pete."

I answered, still a little worried, "OK, cool, what are you guys up to?"

"Well that's the reason I called."

Oh no, I knew it, something had gone wrong, I was selfishly feeling that my great evening had been ruined, but I knew this wasn't about a job, but a relationship and I knew ministry happens during interruptions. So, conflicted as I was, I asked with a genuine tone, "What's going on?"

He said, "Well, we were at this party of some friends of ours and there was a keg and a bunch of liquor and pills, and we just felt really uncomfortable, so we left. It was hard to leave, but we just did it in a respectful way and said we were uncomfortable and wanted to go do something else. So now we are driving around looking for some food and talking about our choices and all of that, you know getting all deep and stuff, and I just felt like I wanted to call you and let you know what happened, to keep us accountable, you know?"

It was one of the coolest things I'd seen in all of my years in youth ministry. The way these guys took a stand on their faith, in one of the hardest places to do it, within their group of peers in the middle of a huge party, was incredible. I told them how proud of them I was, and affirmed how tough of a decision that must have been. Tyler said that Luke had gone with them, but decided he wanted to stay. He really liked this girl there, so they didn't try and make him feel guilty. He told them that he'd be fine and he would call them if he needed a ride home.

I told them, "Those decisions can't be forced. It has to come from a conviction in your heart, which is why you guys made the choice. Your actions are speaking loudly of your faith. I'm really impressed and proud of you guys, let Pete know that too, and take it easy on Luke, he's a good dude and he'll get it figured out."

We hung up and I felt a little bummed out. I was very happy with what was said on the other side of the phone, but I hated that my initial instinct was to assume the worst, which is what I did. I continued to be amazed at how God was showing himself through Tyler and the students; however, I didn't want to be shocked at it, because if I was, then I wasn't giving God enough credit for His power to transform hearts. I sat back down with JoHanna and told her about the conversation. She smiled, and we continued on with our DVD and channel surfing evening.

I'm not sure exactly what time it was when we went to bed. When one of us finally falls asleep in the living room, the other will eventually nudge them to get up and go to bed. That night was my turn to nod out first. I know it was pretty late, by our standards. It might have even pushed midnight! We headed to our bedroom and I fell asleep that night with a comforted, content peace.

—⟋⟍—

The next thing I remember hearing was a loud boom and knocking. It took a second to realize that it wasn't a dream. I popped up and looked at JoHanna, who is a very light sleeper and she looked startled. I said, "What was that?" Thinking I'd give it another chance that it was a dream. She said in a whisper, "I think someone's at our front door!" My instinct wasn't that it was a robber or something; I mean we lived in an apartment building in one of the safest cities in the country. But, I threw a shirt on and still walked cautiously out of our bedroom toward the front door. As I turned the corner into the living room, I heard the banging again, much louder this time, more urgent and along with it I heard voices. It was all very surreal, and as I got to the door I looked out and saw Tyler with a few of his friends, desperately wanting to get inside.

I opened the door, and before I could speak, Tyler and three friends had barged into the living room and sat down anxiously. They kept saying "Oh my God, oh my God!" It almost looked as though they'd just robbed a bank and were looking for cover, questioning what they'd done.

I started to speak, frantically because the situation was so escalated, "Guys, what's going on?!" And as I barely finished the question, I heard Tyler's tone turn from frantic to shock on a dime as he said with a very shaky voice, "Luke died tonight." Not knowing what to say, do, or what exactly had happened, I reached out and Tyler grabbed me in an embrace. The other three friends, one of whom was Pete and the other two who'd been to youth group sat and held each other on the couch. It felt like I held Tyler for ten minutes. He was in shock, I was in shock, and I didn't know what to do or say. I don't care how much training in youth ministry you have or how many times you've dealt with a similar situation, there was nothing you could say or do in a moment like that to make it all right or find the words to fix it. The hug was the only response I could muster, and at that moment the only one necessary.

There were tears and uncontrollable shaking. There were hugs, hand holding and incoherent speaking. JoHanna had turned the corner after hearing this entire conversation taking place and felt just as lost as I did, and just as lost as those kids did. She went to the couch and started holding the two girls in her arms. I still had no idea what they were talking about, what had happened or if any of it was true. What I did know was that something had happened to Luke that night and they had found there way over to my place seeking solace, guidance and answers, but a hug and couch were all I could offer. I didn't have answers, I didn't even know the questions, but I felt absolutely helpless.

After minutes, which seemed like hours of hysterics, I finally said as calmly as I could, "Tell me what happened." Tamara, one of the girls, spoke up first and said, "Luke was shot tonight at that party. I watched it happen! I was standing five feet away from him, Oh GOD, WHY?! WHY?! Oh my…" And then she broke down in tears back into JoHanna's embrace. I felt socked in the stomach at that moment. I was wondering what had happened within those past six or seven hours since I spoke with Tyler on the phone, and felt a sense of guilt, as if I could have stopped it. I was also wondering all of the other tangible things, like how Luke could have been shot to death? That didn't make any sense. My mind was racing as I tried to console a group of kids whose lives I knew would never be the same again. This was a moment that would never be forgotten and it was happening right in my living room.

"We just got back from the hospital; they said he died on the way there in the ambulance," Tyler said. "I can't believe this is happening. Why is this happening?! What is God doing?!!"

I have to admit, I was echoing his exact questions in my own heart as he passionately searched for an explanation. I again was speechless. His words rang so much of rhetoric, as well as brutal honesty. When horrible things happen, that's what we want to know. We want to know WHY! And I couldn't say, especially not in that moment. It wasn't a time to start saying all of the right

"Christian" things, about God has a plan etc. I highly doubt it was God's plan for Luke to get shot to death at a party. There were no answers that night on any level. We spent the next couple of hours in the living room talking, and also sitting in silence. I knew my role in that was to just stay silent and be present. That's what I had to offer and it was all right.

JoHanna had called all of the kids' parents to let them know where they were. As you could imagine they were all very concerned and hurting as well. No one slept that night and by morning when the sun came up I drove all the students home. As we were driving I saw news camera crews passing us all along the street. Apparently there was a bigger story here, and it was making headlines. I was a zombie that morning. Instead of being a rock, I felt like water. My own personal world had been flipped upside down, and as I was trying to retrace the steps and all that had happened the previous night, I picked up the morning paper. It was Sunday and the only day we even got the newspaper. I glanced at the front page and there, already, in a color senior picture was Luke, smiling and holding his soccer ball. I broke down when I read the headline, "Drinking Leads to Accidental Shooting Death of Local Teen." I had no idea what that even meant, it continued to feel like a dream. I was numb. I became even number as I read the story. And as I read I was very conscious that this had all happened within the past ten hours.

The story talked about how there was a teenage drinking party that night and at some point during the party a bunch of the kids were hanging outside on the porch of a large beach house. In the garage there were a couple of guns that belonged to the owner of the house who was out of town. The son, who had thrown the party, picked up one of the hand guns and started carrying it around, while jokingly pointing it at himself and others. He claimed it wasn't loaded. After carelessly pulling the trigger at random people and objects, he set the gun down for awhile and started talking with Luke, who was clueless to what had been happening. The boy then grabbed the gun again a few minutes later and proceeded to put it up to his own head and Luke's, claiming again that it wasn't loaded. There was a mixture among everyone of drunken laughter and concern over what was happening. Then the boy accidentally pulled the trigger, the gun went off. Luke stood up straight for a second and then hunched to the sandy beach next to the deck.

The story described the chaos that ensued as was vividly evident on the 911 recording which the newspaper transcribed. But I could imagine the horror that scene probably looked like. I knew Luke; I had seen Tyler, Pete and the other kids' faces when they came to my house. No matter what else I read, I had the scene already imprinted in my head. In one of the most horrific accidents you can imagine, Luke was gone; a seventeen-year-old high school senior with a great laugh, big heart, a soccer scholarship to UCLA and a beautiful budding relationship with Jesus Christ.

That morning, the church was buzzing. There were many people talking about the incident and a lot of people were learning that Luke was a student in our youth program. People were debating over the details of "Well I heard this…" and weighing in on their personal opinions of teen drinking and all of that, but the bottom line was that a young man's life was over and many others were going to be permanently altered because of a string of poor choices that happened all over the span of a few hours and over a few beers.

There weren't a lot of students at church that morning which surprised me. The ones who were there sat in silence for awhile with me in the youth room as we then proceeded to share memories of Luke and our fresh feelings over what had happened. Again, there weren't words, or right answers.

I don't believe the shooting was God's will, but somehow He ends up taking the blame and I found myself having feelings of resentment and anger toward God as well. And as I was internally struggling, I noticed that neither Tyler nor Pete had come to church that morning and I had to wonder if after everything that happened over that school year, if they would ever show up again. But they did.

I put the word out that I would be in the youth room that evening with some of our other adult leaders to talk and listen, and to my surprise word got around quickly. At about 6 o'clock I got to church and opened all of the doors to the youth wing. And about fifteen minutes later, there were over fifty students in the room. I had probably met twenty of them before. They all came seeking something; they wanted answers, but mostly they all just needed a place to go and be, and even if you're not religious, the church is always a place that feels safe in those situations, I guess.

As we sat around, sharing, staring, crying and pacing, Tyler and Pete showed up. It was well known that those two completed the trilogy of Tyler-Luke-Pete. And as they walked up to the door, they said, "Hey, there's this thing going on at school right now, let's go." There was a vigil being held outside of the gym on the school grounds at the high school. So immediately we all packed up into a caravan of cars and headed over.

I took two students and two adult leaders in my jeep with me. When we pulled up to the school we could hardly find a place to park. I couldn't believe how fast the word had traveled, of not only the accident, but of the specific meeting place and vigil. As we got out of the car and started walking toward the massive crowd I noticed news trucks all over the place. They were interviewing a lot of students and adults. I felt pretty disturbed by it all, it seemed as though they were only looking for a story, with no compassion as they shoved microphones in grieving students' and parents' faces. It was also disturbing to watch some of the TV crew tech guys laughing about random stuff as they posted up against their news van. They were totally oblivious to what was happening around them. It definitely felt like something out of a movie, and I kept thinking we were all on set. But, it was all very real; almost too real to handle.

We got to where the massive crowd was and I took a stand up against a fence toward the back of it all with a couple of our leaders. I was just observing the scene and praying inside over everything that was happening. There was a huge message board of construction paper draped over the fence at the center of the crowd, opposite of where we were standing. I couldn't read much of what it said, but it was covered with memories, thoughts and prayers. And along with that there were many flowers and other items that included Luke's soccer jersey on display.

It was a somber time to say the least. There were small groups of students praying, and I heard a lot of sniffles and wails. There were also a large number of people completely in shock who didn't know how to react. I saw a couple of the other local youth pastors from town that I'd been getting to know and made small talk with them. I could only assume they were feeling the same way inside that I was. I watched as the kids from my youth group consoled each other and reached out to their other friends. I watched Tyler as he stood strong and silent, while continuously receiving hugs from people. I was so broken by that scene. I was worried about him and his faith; knowing that he'd finally made sense of who God was in his life, and now this. I was worried that he was going to turn his back on all of it as he had done in the past. And I'm sure he was asking all the natural questions such as, "How could this happen? Why did this have to happen in my life again?" Those echoing thoughts must have been flowing throughout him and I was hurt. I didn't blame him, and I couldn't answer any of them either. I came to realize those weren't just Tyler's questions, but my own, as I continued to not seek guidance and comfort, but to accuse God and get even more upset.

I stayed around a long time that night, basically until everyone else had left. Before Tyler left I gave him a hug and told him I loved him. I told him that God had this all under control, but as I said it I felt the tension from my words penetrating his heart. It was a sense of cold frustration; not compassion or comfort. He left that night with a few of his friends, but I couldn't leave that scene. I made sure the people who I'd given a ride to found another way home and I stayed around campus. As I continued to walk, not much further than the memorial, I saw the bench that I had sat on that past fall when I had surrendered to God's direction in my life. So I sat down on that same bench and had a fight with God.

I replayed the conversation we'd had on that night that past fall. I knew I was out there for a reason and God was in control. God took me in a direction and had my back throughout all that had happened that school year. I felt like he put me in Tyler's life and Tyler in mine. I had felt a distinct reasoning for that direction, one that I was trying to teach those students to seek out in their own lives, and all I could question at that time, was, "Is this how it all works out?" I couldn't help but think it was all built up to be totally broken down, and the toll it must be taking in Tyler's life. I realized God never promised a sorrow or pain-free life, but I couldn't make sense of it all, and didn't even want to try. I felt as if in that moment, when I was expected to be a strong leader and comfort everyone else, that I was ready to give up. I wanted to leave ministry, I didn't want to build anymore relationships with students because that kind of thing happens. And the more students I knew, eventually, the more hurt and pain I'd have to suffer through with them, and I just didn't think I was strong enough to handle that. Did God even understand?

I couldn't help the way I was grieving with it all. I couldn't act like it hadn't affected me deeply. I felt I couldn't be the caregiver I strongly thought I needed to be. And so I sat there for a couple hours, pondering what my life would have looked like if I didn't ever get into ministry. I thought about what if I was doing something wrong? I wondered if I could've saved him, and I wondered what the fastest highway out of California was, because I was ready to run away.

1 7

Aftershock

"When we honestly ask ourselves which person in our lives mean the most to us, we often find that it is those who, instead of giving advice, solutions, or cures, have chosen rather to share our pain and touch our wounds with a warm and tender hand. The friend who can be silent with us in a moment of despair or confusion, who can stay with us in an hour of grief and bereavement, who can tolerate not knowing, not curing, not healing and face with us the reality of our powerlessness, that is a friend who cares."

— Henri J.M. Nouwen
The Road to Daybreak:
A Spiritual Journey

Those next few days following Luke's death were very hard. It was all starting to sink in for everyone, especially that next day when the students all went back to school. The memorial stayed up for the entire week and there was constant traffic to the counseling center as they brought in local pastors and youth pastors to be available for the kids. I was asked to be a part of it, but told them to use me on an as-needed basis. I didn't even know what I meant by that since there was obviously a glaring need, however I knew I couldn't fully commit to being a part of it, at least not at the moment. I was still worrying about how to nurture my own students at church, as well as my own feelings.

Some students couldn't even go back to school yet; it was just too hard for them. And as I suspected, the story was all over the news reports for the next few days. It seemed that I couldn't turn on the news without seeing Luke's face, or the familiar faces of people and kids that I knew. Luke's friend, Cory, was even interviewed on one station. He looked so lost and distraught, as if he hadn't slept since the night it happened. The only thing he could say was, "Last Friday I was sitting by him at lunch, and now I'm never going to see him again." It was painful to face those realities.

The news stations and local papers continued to use the story as an example. They kept bringing up the problems with teen drinking and parents being enablers and all of those things that seemed secondary. Everyone was trying to put the blame somewhere and people who were completely outside of the situation felt an obligation or right to chime in with their own insensitive thoughts condemning it. They would say things like, "Well, that's what happens when kids aren't responsible" and "It's too bad kids these days think they need to have alcohol to have fun because this is what happens…" etc.

That made me even more upset. The focus was turned away from the goodness in Luke's life and it seemed they were using this accident as a pedestal for people to spout off their opinions about everything. I kept thinking what it must have been like for

Luke's mom and dad to read those things. To me, those people were all missing the point. What those students needed wasn't another seminar teaching them that teen drinking was dangerous or that you shouldn't drive while drinking, or in this case pull out a handgun. The real issues here went a lot deeper.

I obviously don't condone teen drinking, but I believe the reason for it goes much deeper into the heart of how stressful life can be and in a lot of situations, how alone or unloved a kid can feel at times. Therefore, drinking, drugs and other stimulants are merely outlets for a deeper longing. And that longing is one I know Jesus came to offer a better way of living for! By people investing into the lives of these youth, caring about them and listening to them, I think their self-esteem and worth can be significantly enhanced. And that's not only for kids, that's for everyone in life. We are all wired with a desire to be cared for, listened to and wanted. As much as Jesus came to offer that, we have the responsibility as followers of Christ to offer that physically to others, just as He has taught. The bottom line for me is that it's more important to realize and help the deeper cause of the decision rather than only focus on the end result. And in this case, the end result was devastating.

———ɯ———

The funeral took place a couple of days later. It was held at the large Catholic Church in town, not because that's where Luke's family went, but because it was the only place that would hold the mass number of people who attended. I'm not sure of the exact number, but it was at least 1,500. And out of those, many didn't even know Luke very well, but were classmates and neighbors who were there to show respect and support for his family. JoHanna and I arrived a little late to the funeral. It hadn't started yet, but there wasn't anywhere to sit. You had the feeling that the words "Fire Code" meant nothing in the church that day after seeing people lining up all throughout the aisles. JoHanna and I found a spot near the back and leaned up against the wall. A few minutes later the pallbearers walked the casket down the center aisle. Tyler was in the front on the right side, the same side that we were standing on. I had never seen him so formal or dressed up.

The funeral began and a few friends had a chance to share, as well as Luke's older sister. They all spoke well, but were very tough to listen to. The Luke they were talking about was one who was fully alive, yet the reality now was that his broken body lay in a casket in front of 1,500 people. It was a clear message of the fine line between sorrow and the hope we have in Christ.

A couple of things were running through my mind during the funeral. The first one was that I kept wondering if that many people would show up at my funeral? It wasn't in a selfish way or a competition, but I was really wondering if that many people would care about me. The other thing I was pondering was what was next in my life? While trying to lean on God for comfort and guidance, I was still struggling with recognizing His will and continued to worry about what this was all doing to the lives of the students who wanted answers, and in particular, Tyler.

After the funeral, I gave some hugs out to kids and as we were walking out the door, I was stopped. It was Luke's mom. She put her hand gently on my arm and said, "You're Evan, right?" I had smiled at her once during a soccer game, but hadn't seen her again until that day at her son's funeral. I said, "Yes." She gave me a hug and told me that Luke really appreciated me and they'd seen a great change in him over the last couple of months. I didn't know how to respond or take that. I hadn't realized the impact I had had on Luke's life. My only response to her was, "Thank you, he was an awesome kid, I'm so sorry." For a guy that likes to talk as much as I do, getting into a position where there aren't many words to say is tough. And also, being in a situation I can't solve or fix for those who are hurting, is even harder. We left the church that day as I continued to struggle with my own faith.

18

The Student Becomes the Teacher

"The Bible tells a story. A story that isn't over.
A story that is still being told.
A story that we have a part to play in."
–Rob Bell, *Velvet Elvis*

Although things had changed in many ways forever in our town, some sort of normalcy had returned over the next couple of weeks. One thing that had changed however, was that I hadn't seen Tyler back at church. There were a lot of students who continued to come and hang around, but he wasn't one of them. I knew he needed space, and so to be respectful of that, I tried not to call him. Although that didn't mean I had stopped worrying about him.

We dedicated a lot of time during our youth group discussions to focus on talking about grief. I invited our Associate Pastor in to share and talk things over and he did it much better than I ever could. During those discussions I spent most of the time listening and being an outlet. My compassion and love for the kids hadn't changed, although I continued to struggle with focus and direction myself. I think that was part of the problem and why the accident was affecting me so greatly. I wanted so much to be all right with it and wanted to see the kids that I loved be all right with it too, and I knew it wouldn't come from my own power or understanding. But I wasn't able or willing to let God take that over. In other terms, you could say I was *spiritually frustrated.*

JoHanna heard the most of it. I couldn't fake anything around her, because if I did, she would call me out anyway, so I never tried. That's what made our relationship so solid. She consoled me as much as possible, but she was dealing with her own set of problems and circumstances. She was trying to build me up in whatever way she could, even though I hadn't always done the same for her.

I felt as though my funnel was drained completely and there was not a drop of anything coming in the top. So because of that, I stopped trying so hard and shut down my engine for a few days, hoping to get back into at least neutral before I even thought about driving again. I did the most blasphemous thing I could do; I called in sick to work.

I was sick though, in many ways. I was mentally and physically drained, but more importantly, spiritually drained. The next couple of days I just laid around the house. And during that time I didn't try to soul search, I wasn't seeking anything, I only wanted to be. I wanted to be alone, and I wanted to watch *Saved by the Bell* reruns all day. I kept trying to figure out how it was possible for Zack and Slater to play so many different sports in one high school year, and also why they always seemed to be juniors or seniors, but never graduated when they were supposed to. Let's face it; the show was on for five years of high school, what was up with that?

Yes, those were the thoughts consuming my life for those couple of days. I ate a lot of Doritos and drank a lot of soda, when I had an appetite, and just let myself lose touch with reality. My plan was to escape from it all for awhile. Those were a good couple of days because I would wake up an average of three times a day due to my naps. After awhile, I got myself at least back to a place where I felt I could function again. Thankfully, everyone at church who knew me understood and I got no questioning from any of the staff and felt no guilt. I went back to work at the end of the week.

The day I got back into the office I had about fifteen voicemails and one hundred e-mails. So of course, instead of checking all of those, I went to the 7-eleven to get a couple of donuts. As I was driving over there Tyler called me. I didn't answer since I was driving responsibly, but I called him back as soon as I parked.

"Hey Evan," Tyler said as he picked up my call back.

"Hey, what's goin' on? How are you doing my man?"

"I'm hanging in there all right," he said. "How are things with you? I heard you were sick. I tried stopping by church the other day and they said you were at home chillin'."

I responded and downplayed it a little, "Yeah, I just felt a little exhausted and needed a couple days to recoup."

"Oh tight, well hope you're better, I was kinda concerned," Tyler said with a very loving tone. I was shocked that he would even be thinking that way, but he definitely called out my bluff. I sensed he knew something more was going on with me. He was a lot more intuitive than I probably gave him credit for. Then he asked if we could meet up that week and told me he wanted to talk. I of course said yes, but was feeling nervous about it knowing that I didn't have any advice or anything to offer him. He named the place and time and I told him I'd pick him up there.

I didn't know what to expect when I picked Tyler up that Saturday morning. It had now been two weeks since Luke died and I hadn't really spoken with or seen him since the night he showed up on my doorstep and that following night at school. I was anxious and had all of the symptoms, but also had an eagerness to hear what was on his mind. And as we drove that twenty minute drive to the beach, it was obvious that we didn't even know where to begin, and so we did what any guys would do in that semi-uncomfortable situation; we talked about sports. That was always a good constant. It was springtime and baseball had recently started, so we talked about that. I took a little time to rouse him for his football picks that didn't quite pan out that year. Mine didn't either, but I defended them much better than he did. It was always that competition within the competition that was the most fun anyway, the bickering and justifying stuff that we ultimately had no control over.

The distraction of sports talk got us back on the same page it felt, and although those had been two of the hardest weeks in Tyler's life, he appeared a lot more optimistic and level-headed than I had expected. He must have seen the opposite in me because after we grabbed some slushies and candy, yes at 9:30 in the morning, and sat down at the beach in a secluded area about twenty feet from the water he started to speak softly.

Tyler: Hey man, you all right?
Evan: I'm doing all right, how are you?
T: Things have been crazy and hard, that's for sure, but I'm doing all right with stuff.

(We both knew what "stuff" he was referring to.)
After a long pause…

T: I keep replaying that night in my mind. I keep picturing Luke's face and wondering if I could've done more to save him from that party. I keep thinking, if I had only done this or that, then he'd still be alive. It's the same feelings I felt when my brother died.
E: Yeah, but you know, you can't think that way. It wasn't your fault and although we don't always know why things happen the way that they do, they… (I stopped.)

Tyler stared at me like he was ready to call me out. He asked me if I even believed what I was saying. He told me that he'd heard it before.
I broke down and said to him;

E: I'm not sure what to believe to be honest Tyler. This has been a huge test for me. I feel so terrible about Luke's death and what you've been through. I've been fighting with God. I've been praying and hoping that your faith isn't lost because of all of this, but I wouldn't blame you if it was. I've been contemplating my own beliefs to be truly honest.

Tyler paused for a second before he starting speaking again. And then, instead of joining in my sorrow and complaining, he started grinning. He said to me the same words that I'd spoken to him at camp months before, "God can handle it, God can handle it, God can handle it." I looked at his reassuring smile. It wasn't sarcastic, it was completely compassionate. Then he spoke again, words that shook my world.

T: I've been reading my Bible a lot lately. I was reading this story about Lazarus. He was Jesus' friend and he had

died. Jesus came to see him, and when He saw him it says that "Jesus Wept" (John 11:35). He cried and grieved over his friend and it said that he was "deeply moved." But like moments later he raised him from the dead back to life! It's crazy 'cause even though he knew that a minute later he would be with his buddy again, in the moment he had sorrow and grief. He showed he was human and God all at the same time. And I love that story. Jesus had the power to totally overcome death and he's done that! How tight is that?! Check this verse out, "Did I not tell you that if you believed, you would see the glory of God?" (John 11:40)

I couldn't believe what I was hearing. Tyler's tone and voice were almost of excitement when he spoke about what Jesus had done. He was explaining to me a story that I'd heard many times, but this time it became real and the story meant something that I hadn't thought of before. Then he continued…

T: I know that after my brother died, I tried to make sense of everything. The why, the guilt and all of those feelings that I couldn't explain and didn't want to deal with. But I learned, with your help, that we don't always need to know the answers and that *God's love is greater than our own circumstances.* We don't need to know why everything happens the way it does. We just gotta trust God and know that He is holding it all in His hands. We need to have the faith to know and trust that there are certain things we can't control and to just know that God works good through all things. He works them to good, but isn't always responsible for the bad stuff that happens, you know what I'm saying? I was so upset when my brother drowned and might always be, but I don't blame God. If anything it makes me cling to Him more. I've learned that there's a big difference between God causing things to happen, and God allowing things to

happen…

He was speaking to my soul. This kid that I'd known for less than a year was teaching me about life and faith. I was wondering how I could have been so self-centered to think that it was all about me and to believe that God maybe wasn't working in this whole thing after all. I was captivated and drawn in by his words. Here I was so worried Tyler would lose his faith and turn away from God and that I didn't have the words to speak to him. And what I really needed all along was to just shut up and listen. I was the one who turned away.

T: I know that you feel pretty bad and guilty about stuff. And I have just had this feeling in my heart for the past week that God wanted me to talk to you.

Truer words could not have been spoken.
Tyler ended by saying, **Evan, this life isn't about us. You taught me to seek out Jesus and seek out God's teaching. That's one thing that's clear. Luke is gone, but our own stories will continue on and we need to be a part of that.** *This isn't over.*
He then opened up the small Bible that he'd had stuffed in his pocket and read; "Therefore, there is now no condemnation for those who are in Christ Jesus" (Rom. 8:1) and "Trust in the LORD with all your heart and lean not on your own understanding; in all your ways acknowledge him, and he will make your paths straight" (Prov. 3:5).
T: Evan, *this isn't over.* **I sort of feel like it's all just starting…**

I knew exactly what he meant. I tried to speak, but the only way I could respond in that moment was tears. I let them fly. As I sat there humbled by Tyler's words, I realized that God's grace was breaking me down. It was breaking down the limits of my understanding and stubbornness and showing me the eternal and infinite limits of mercy and love. I fell in love with God again on the beach through the eyes of a high school student.

—ɯ—

Those next few weeks seemed to move by quickly. They were tough in a lot of ways, but positive in many ways as well. It was springtime and school was almost over. The days were getting later and our crowds at church kept growing, even if there were those kids who would only come for the dodgeball and video games part of the night and bail as soon as we started heading inside. But, I got smart to the game a little and some nights we'd set up our talking and message time in the parking lot or in the grassy area on the church property. That's what Jesus would've done anyway, right? He didn't need a PowerPoint presentation. I loved what I was doing, and I loved what God was doing in and through me. When you fight in any relationship, if it doesn't end up breaking, it only makes it stronger. My faith and love for God was as strong as it had ever been that spring. I realized what I already thought I knew, that life is meant to be lived glorifying God and what is most important are the relationships we have.

I had heard that in ministry you need to give it at least a year to really get a good read on your situation and to be fully comfortable. I had done that. I was coming to the end of my first full school year and I knew that I needed to stay and I was supposed to be there. I remembered thinking that previous fall, that I could have just gotten up and left and no one would've noticed, and I would have forgotten too. But, I knew at that point, it wasn't true anymore.

It was a great spring in California. Prom came and went, and my wife was asked by four different high school boys from the youth group, respectfully declining each invitation. We were also looking to move into a nicer place, a guest house with a yard that was closer to the church. We even adopted a wiener dog! Things were moving in the right direction. Despite life's struggles, things go on. I learned that life is all about how we react and respond to our situations, regardless if they are good or bad. It's what makes us who we are, and having that faith in Christ, we know the outcome. It's like when I was watching the movie *Miracle*. It is a true story, yet I watched it with such anxiety and anticipation, as if I didn't know the end result! They beat the Russian team, and I even knew what the final score was going to be while watching the movie. That is how life is when we have Christ. We tend to get caught up in the craziness of routine with stress and worries, but we know how it ends. And when we know that, it should take away those things that hold us down and allow us the freedom to live a life of love to the highest degree of fulfillment and purpose!

Even though we had settled down, there was always transitioning going on around us. Our worship director at church was leaving at the end of that summer, and I had grown very close to her. Along with that, we had a lot of students now who were graduating from our program and heading off to college to change the world.

Tyler was one of those who was leaving. It was hard to see him go, but had been such a blessing to see him come to faith. I hoped he'd continue growing in his faith as he headed to San Diego that fall. He was going to go to a small school where he could pursue a business degree. We had him over to our house the last night before he moved away to school. We stayed up late and shared funny stories and reflected on the past year. He told me he never would have pictured his life like it was at that point, a year earlier. "I was on a selfish path to destruction, but now I feel that life is worthwhile," he said.

We had a big man hug and said goodbye. He was one out of the many students who I had met over the years that I knew I would keep contact with for a long time. Over the next year we kept in contact through e-mails, texting and the occasional phone call. He came home at Christmas time, but other than that, he didn't head back too often. Not to mention I was concentrating a lot on the students who were still around town and in the youth program.

I coached again that year and was heavily involved and invested in making that year as powerful and meaningful as the previous one. Tyler's influence and life transformation lived on through the friends, school, and community that he inspired through his example.

19

A Revolution

"As a rock star, I have two instincts, I want to have
fun, and I want to change the world. I have a chance
to do both."
– Bono

"God has created each of us with a unique
contribution to make to our world and to our times.
No other person has our same abilities, motivations,
network of friends and relationships, perspectives,
ideas, or experiences. When we, like misplaced
puzzle pieces, fail to show up, the overall picture is
diminished."
– Richard Stearns, *The Hole in Our Gospel*

A few years had gone by since we moved to California and I started working at my church. I felt for awhile that God had been calling me away to do something else. So, after I finished my fourth school year there, JoHanna and I moved on. We went to an area about an hour and a half away from where we were. It was far enough away to allow us to move on and forward, but not too far that we couldn't maintain the friendships and relationships we had made over those four years.

It was tough to leave and say goodbye, but everyone was so encouraging and understanding.

And as for Tyler, I hadn't talked to him in a long time. We'd hit each other up on Facebook every few months or so. The last I heard he had dropped out of business school to try and become a helicopter pilot and after that didn't work out he went on a three month trip to Ireland.

I thought about those kids a lot. Youth ministry isn't the type of job where you can just leave and be done with it. I did that with the restaurant business as well as retail jobs that I had along the way, but ministry is all about relationships and so there's a certain level of grieving and closure that needs to take place when you are removed from that situation. It was hard and emotional, but it was also good and we had moved on.

It was Christmas Day that year in our new place in California. We didn't have any plans with family and were new to our current area so we decided we didn't want to break the tradition that we started three years prior, so we drove to Venice Beach to spend the day strolling along the boardwalk. It was an hour and a half drive from where we lived now, but we filled the car time with eighties music and conversation.

We got to the beach and parked a little ways away from the boardwalk because we wanted to avoid paying the seven bucks they charged in the lot. I wondered why, on Christmas of all days, they couldn't just give parking out as a gift? But it felt good to see that familiar beach and wander around the little shops. The street performers and artists were all out in full force that day too. It was a beautiful day of walking and relaxation.

As we continued to walk we noticed that we were seeing a lot of people who had black backpacks on and were wearing shirts that said, "It's Only A Candy Bar." That obviously caught our eye as much as it caught the eyes of many of the people out that day. I noticed that most of the people with the backpacks seemed to be hanging out with all of the homeless crowds who were gathered by the sand and along the boardwalk. Those were the crowds of people that JoHanna and I always wanted to go talk to, but were intimidated by not knowing exactly what to say or how to approach them. There always seemed to be an excuse in our minds not to, which made it even cooler to see these people interacting so easily with them.

Curiosity finally got the best of me, and so when a girl and guy, who were probably in their mid-twenties walked by us, I stopped them and asked, "Hey, so tell me about this, what are you guys doing?"

The girl spoke up and said, "We're serving with 'It's Only A Candy Bar'. It's a mission organization that brings the simple things to people in need, but even more than that, we focus on building relationships with people who are lost and hurting."

That sounded amazing, to see people who were being the hands and feet of Christ walking around sharing love. And so I asked them what was in the backpacks. The guy answered this time and said, "We fill them with socks, soda, winter hats, blankets, and of course candy bars and treats. We also spend time with the people we meet, and ask them how they are doing and if they could share their stories with us, which most people are eager to do."

JoHanna interrupted with excitement and said, "Yeah, I just saw something on the news about this the other day, it's getting to be a pretty huge movement."

He continued, as he briefly acknowledged her comment, "Yeah, and it's great to just listen to people talk. Then we'll usually have an opportunity to share our own stories with them, and if we're lucky, we can spend a few minutes lifting them up in prayer and just hanging out with them. See that group over there (he pointed)? They have been singing Christmas Carols and playing the guitar for about a half hour now."

I thought about how incredible that was. It wasn't just people going around handing out Bibles thinking that was good enough, but people who were investing their time, sharing stories and truly being Christ to others, showing them the worth that Jesus would've shown them. I was inspired. It's something that I would want to do, and I wondered how I could be a part of it. It's the kind of thing that I was drawn into because of its realness, which is the same for the Kingdom of God, and that's exactly what this looked like.

As we looked around, there seemed to be more people and backpacks all over the place, but as we walked closer to that circle of new friends singing carols, I noticed all of the smiles on the faces of everyone involved and felt for that moment, this is what heaven must look like.

We had just about made it to the edge of the ever-growing circle and crowd when I heard someone shout my name. I turned around and didn't see anything. I looked at JoHanna and turned back around after giving the "Who knows?" face. Within a second of turning around I felt a huge embrace from behind that about knocked me over. I turned around, in almost a defensive manner, thinking I was getting mugged or something and looked into the eyes of the smiling face of Tyler! I couldn't believe it! He then gave me another huge hug. He gave JoHanna one as well as we stood there shocked to see each other.

"Hey! What are you doing here?!" was the first logical question I could spit out. But even as I said it, I looked at his "It's Only A Candy Bar" shirt and I already knew. He started to speak, but I stopped him and said, "Wait, you're with the candy bar people?"

He said, "Yeah, how did you know?"

"Well, your shirt for one (sarcastically), no, we just talked with a couple of people who you are working with, this is such a great idea!"

We walked a little ways away from the excitement and noise and walked along the beach. Tyler filled us in on life, and we did the same. And after a little while of doing that, I brought it back to the "Candy Bar" thing. "So, what's up with this whole organization?" Tyler looked almost shy as he said, "Well, it was something that I just felt motivated to start, you know?"

"What?!! You started this thing?!" I yelled in amazement.

Tyler started explaining and he got more filled with passion by every word he spoke, as though he had been holding this great idea in for so long, and now it was a reality.

So, do you remember back when I was a senior and we went to the rescue mission downtown? he asked. Of course I remembered, but I remembered thinking that he didn't care much about that day. Boy was I wrong. Standing corrected with every word he continued to say.

> *That day was the first time I had ever done anything like that. I was pretty uncomfortable and nervous, and didn't have a very good attitude. But I remember when we all went up on the roof. I was looking into the crowds of people that lined the streets and kept thinking "they are all people," but it felt more like a zoo or jail and they were trapped prisoners. As I was up there I saw two little kids fighting. They had to be about five years old and they were fighting over a candy bar! A candy bar! And I won't forget the look of satisfaction and relief on the face of the boy who was able to finally wrestle it away from the other one and start eating it, and also the*

hurt on the face of the boy who didn't get it. I kept thinking to myself, "Dude, I just ate two candy bars today and didn't think anything of it, I would love to give them one right now to stop the fighting, I mean it's only a candy bar." My heart broke that day. I couldn't shake that image. If all it would take is a candy bar to provide such joy and hope, how much more would a candy bar and a conversation do? A candy bar and Christ? I have been seeking out a way over the past four years to impact the world and God has kept calling me to start this outreach. I've been preparing it in my heart for years and it's been so amazing to see it in action and to see lives changed through it!

Evan, you asked me once in high school, "How do you want your life to matter?" This is how. This is my answer to that question I spent years thinking about...

At that moment, I couldn't really describe the feelings I had. Here was a kid who was as messed up as the rest of us and using his passions and gifts to reach out to people that our society counts as lost, or doesn't count at all. My only reaction was to give him a hug, and say, "That's the most inspiring thing I've ever heard."

Tyler looked at me with a very serious and sincere face and said, "Evan, dude, you know you saved my life by investing in it and introducing me to Christ. You reached out to me and gave me the future, hope and vision that God created in me, which let's face it, I wasn't looking to find on my own."

I looked him in the eyes and said, "I'm not sure if you ever knew or realized your impact on me. You honestly saved my call to ministry and even my own faith and direction in God."

We smiled and gave one more bro-hug. JoHanna stood there with emotion welling up as if she'd just watched *Old Yeller* or *Titanic*. She broke down as we had a triple embrace. It was real and honest, all of it, not just that moment. As we started laughing with the joy that had overcome us and as I continued to be inspired by a kid who was living out the gospel of Jesus Christ, I said to Tyler, "Now, hook us up with some of those backpacks…"

Vision of Heaven
By Evan Gratz

There's a passion and desire inside of me that leads me to
plunge into the depths of a body of water that has no end.
The water is alive and I am still.
I have a fullness of breath that I haven't felt before.
I am still as I look up to see my creator reaching down.
My hand touches a scar and I am brought to a place that
I've never seen. A throne that is too bright to look at.
The passion and longing turns to a peace only felt in the
presence of a father and a son.
I lay down.
I see only a ray of light shining on me, like a spotlight from
the throne.
I hear songs that I've never heard, but I'm singing along.
The scarred hand reaches out to me, picks me up and I'm
sitting at a table with Jesus.
I can't speak, and my eyes go directly back to the hands
that rescued me, to see the scars have disappeared. My
savior looks at me with the warmest, most welcoming smile
and says, "It's all finished, welcome home."
I fall asleep in His arms only to awake in a green pasture.
It's the Garden of Eden. Everything has been restored.
I have no fears, and I am not sick. I have no memory of
anything. There is no guilt and no regrets. The waters are
beautiful. There is a tree. There is no judgment. I see a
sheep that runs by. Jesus glances at the sheep, looks back at
me, and smiles knowingly.
Again, He says to me:
"Welcome home, I've been waiting for you..."

Questions to Ponder and Discuss

Chapter 1

1. When was a time in your life where you took a leap of faith when you heard God calling?

2. How do you deal with transition and change?

3. Think about a time when you were in a significant transition in life. How did it feel and what was good and bad about it?

Chapter 2

1. Do you feel settled and grounded in life?

2. What are the things that make you feel that way?

3. Are you content in your current situation in life? Why or why not?

Chapter 3

1. Have you ever invited Jesus to be a part of your daily life and activities?

2. How would your life look different if you did?

3. Is there something that needs to change in your heart right now? What is it?

Chapter 4

1. What are you passionate about and who do you trust to be part of that passion?

2. If you are a student, what adults do you relate to the best and why? What are the qualities that draw you in?

3. If you are a leader or adult, how do you best relate to students? In what ways are you intentional about that?

4. Have you ever pictured Jesus as a friend and a real person in your life? Or is He only a spirit of imagination? How *real* is He to you?

Chapter 5

1. What do the words "reaching out" or "outreach" mean to you?

2. Are there ways in your life where you do that? How?

3. Why is outreach important?

4. How do you deal with unrealistic expectations or miscommunication when you know in your heart you're doing the right thing?

Chapter 6

1. What things fill your funnel? How do you get fueled and filled up as a person?

2. What are the things that drain your funnel? What drains you of your time and energy?

3. Which "C" word intimidates you the most? Commitment, Christ, Christianity, Church or Compare? Why is that?

4. How are those "C" words perceived? How are they different and how are they related?

5. How do you prioritize your passions? What needs to get the most attention in your life? What actually gets the most attention?

Chapter 7

1. What was something you had really anticipated going to?

2. What is something right now you are really anticipating going to?

3. What are and were your expectations for those things? Did they pan out how you thought? Or if it's in the future, what are your expectations?

Chapter 8

1. Have you ever gone to a camp, Christian or non-Christian camp? What was your experience like? What are your best memories?

2. What is your image of God and His love? Where did that come from? Reading the Bible for yourself? A teacher or pastor? Hear-say from people? Your own assumptions?

3. How did this chapter help shape that image and did you see it in a different way than you have previously? What questions do you have about God?

4. Think about the best faith conversation you've ever had about God, what was that like? If you haven't ever thought about it, what would it look like? What importance would you see in that?

5. Do you *know* that God loves you? Why or why not? Do you *feel* that God loves you? Why or why not?

Chapter 9

1. What has been one of the best team experiences of your life, in any capacity?

2. Are you someone who bottles things up and doesn't let out feelings or search for outlets? Or do you wear your feelings on your sleeve? How do your feelings come out when they do?

3. Have you ever argued or gotten mad at God? Is that OK?

4. When was a time where you've felt very vulnerable?

5. If you were being honest, in what ways are you "sick" in life?

6. Simply asked, "Do you want to get better"? How would you respond?

Chapter 10

1. When was a time in your life that you had an amazing experience, but felt others didn't completely understand your excitement or give you the response you wanted?

2. If you are a Christian, when and how did you decide that? Was it a process or one moment?

3. If you aren't a Christian, what are some reasons you have for not believing in Christ? And what do you believe and why?

4. Do your reasons for being or not being a Christian have anything to do with God? How and why? If not, what is your faith based on?

5. How would you define truth?

Chapter 11

1. What are your biggest questions regarding the Christian faith? How have you found answers, or are you still seeking those?

2. How important do you think it is to seek those answers?

3. What happens when you die? Do you think you get to make it up? If so, why do you think that? If not, what are the options?

4. Do you have more control over where you will go when you die as opposed to choosing to enter the world to begin with? Why?

Chapter 12

1. What are some of the positive and negative perceptions surrounding churches?

2. What do you think churches should look like and be about?

3. When was there a time in your life that you received some shocking bad news? How did you react and how did you feel?

4. How did it end up, or is it something that is still lingering?

Chapter 13

1. How would you define your "Comfort Zone"?

2. When was a time that you had to venture out of that? Was it by choice or was it forced? How did you feel?

3. What does serving look like to you? In what ways do you serve others? Why is that important? Who and how are Christians called to serve?

4. As a human, what is something that breaks your heart to see? How are you responding to that, or do you? If not, why not?

Chapter 14

1. In what ways can serving be done on a large scale? Small scale? Are both equally important in God's eyes?

2. Have you ever thought of your own personal life as a story? As a role in a bigger story?

3. How do you feel knowing that God is telling His story through you? Are you a good story-teller?

4. "Your Life might be the only Bible that someone reads". What does that mean to you? And how might you live differently knowing that's the case?

Chapter 15

1. Do you have a network of friends where you are at now? How do they help inspire or support you? Can you be real around them?

2. Have you ever shared the story of your life with anyone? To who? How did you tell it?

3. Where do you put your faith? In God? In other things? In the idea of no God?

4. Do you feel that your story matters? Why or why not? Is your story even about you?

Chapter 16

1. Think about a time you have had to deal with tragedy. What happened?

2. How did you respond to tragedy? What were the emotions you felt and how did you show them?

3. Does God cause tragedy to happen?

4. What is the difference between "causing" something or "allowing" something? How does God fit into that?

Chapter 17

1. Have you ever attended a funeral? What was that experience like?

2. Is a funeral more about a celebration of life or a somber ending? What is the difference?

3. If you were being honest, have you been to a funeral where you knew for sure that person went to heaven? But then at other times for someone else, maybe weren't sure and were uneasy about it? Why did you feel differently?

4. Can we just assume that everyone goes to heaven? Why or why not? Do we have the right and power to say who goes and who doesn't? Do we have the power to choose where we'll end up?

Chapter 18

1. When was a time where you lost faith in something? Either God or something else. How did you deal with it?

2. Do you believe God can speak through anyone? Including a high school student?

3. Do you believe that "God's love is greater than our own circumstances?"

4. Even through tragedy, when you hear that "This isn't over", does that give you hope?

Chapter 19

1. How have you had to deal with losing touch with someone close to you who's moved away?

2. In what way would you want to see the world change and how could you be the one who leads that charge?

3. Do you feel God calling you to DO SOMETHING in the world right now?

4. In what ways do you want your life to matter? How will you live that out?

**Intermedia
Publishing Group**
Publishing That Works For You

Do you need a speaker?

Do you want Evan Gratz to speak to your group or event? Then contact Larry Davis at: (623) 337-8710 or email: ldavis@intermediapr.com or use the contact form at: www.intermediapr.com.

Whether you want to purchase bulk copies of *It's Only A Candy Bar* or buy another book for a friend, get it now at: www.imprbooks.com.

If you have a book that you would like to publish, contact Terry Whalin, Publisher, at Intermedia Publishing Group, (623) 337-8710 or email: twhalin@intermediapub.com or use the contact form at: www.intermediapub.com.